The Big Book of Wedding Speeches

The Big Book of Wedding Speeches

First published in 2005
by Octopus Publishing Group
2–4 Heron Quays
London E14 4JP
www.conran-octopus.co.uk

Written for Confetti by Sticky Content Ltd
Text copyright © 2005 Confetti Network Ltd;
Book design and layout copyright © 2005 Conran Octopus Ltd;
Illustrations copyright © 2005 Confetti Network Ltd

A catalogue record for this book is available from
the British Library.

ISBN 1 84091 432 7

Publishing Director *Lorraine Dickey*
Editor *Sybella Marlow*
Designer *Jeremy Tilston*
Production Manager *Angela Couchman*

Other books in this series include:
How to Write a Wedding Speech
Speeches
The Best Man's Speech
Jokes, Toasts & One-liners for Wedding Speeches
Wedding Readings & Vows
The Wedding Book of Calm

Contents

Let's be honest here: there are three things most guests remember about a wedding. What the bride wore; how long they had to wait before eating... and how good the speeches were.

If the last item on that list fills you with dread, then chances are you're lined up to speak at your own wedding, or that of a daughter, son or friend. Never fear, Confetti is here to help.

Before you get too stressed at the prospect, put your speech into perspective. True, you'll be the centre of attention for five minutes or so, but the day really belongs to the couple, and most of the time everyone will be focusing on them. The trick is to make your five minutes really count.

Of course, you will need to add your own personal touches, anecdotes and asides. But we hope the following will give you lots of ideas.

Few people are practised in the art of public speaking, so the thought of standing up in front of everyone at a wedding reception and sounding good is pretty intimidating. But don't panic. We have all the advice you need for preparing and making your speech.

Who speaks and when

Traditionally, the toastmaster or master of ceremonies will introduce the speeches at the end of the meal. The formal order of speakers is:

• Father of the bride (or a close family friend)
• The groom
• The best man

But if the bride, chief bridesmaid or guests want to speak, that's great, too!
Traditionally, the speeches take place after the meal, but some couples decide to have them beforehand to allow the speakers to enjoy their meal free of nerves.

The basics

• Firstly, don't panic. A little careful planning will help you deliver a speech that you'll be proud of.
• If you can, visit the reception venue to get an idea of where you'll be standing and the size of the room.
• You will need to project your voice, so practise speaking out loud.
• Find out if you are expected to say a few words and then propose a toast, or to make a long speech.

- Is the reception going to have a theme that you could refer to in your speech or even incorporate into it?
- Are you responsible for presenting gifts to members of the wedding party?
- Find out a little about the guests and if there are any subjects you should avoid.
- How many guests will there be? As a general rule, the more people present, the more formal the speech.

Who says what?

Here is a brief outline of who says what. For more details and for sample speeches, turn to the relevant chapters.

Father of the bride or friend of the family

- Thanks the guests for coming and participating in the special day.
- Thanks everyone who has contributed to the cost of the wedding.
- Compliments and praises the bride, and welcomes her new husband into the family.
- Toasts the bride and groom.

Bridegroom

- Thanks the father of the bride for his toast.
- Thanks the guests for attending and for their gifts.
- Thanks both sets of parents.
- Compliments his bride.
- Thanks his best man.
- Thanks and toasts the bridesmaids.

Best man

- Thanks the groom for his toast to the bridesmaids.
- Comments on the bridal couple, particularly the groom.
- Reads any messages from absent friends and relatives.
- Toasts the bride and groom.

Bride

- Thanks the guests for coming.
- Thanks her parents and bridesmaids.
- Compliments the groom.
- Proposes a toast.

Chief bridesmaid

- Thanks the bride.
- Compliments the ushers.
- Proposes a toast.

Planning your speech

- First, decide whether you want to write out your speech and read it word for word, or memorize it completely, or simply compile a list of bullet points to prompt you.
- Start by noting suitable headings to focus on, then fill in the spaces to produce an entire speech.
- All wedding speeches are just extended toasts, so don't worry that yours has to be worthy of an Oscar winner.
- Make your speech relevant to all the guests, some of whom may not know the bride and groom very well.
- Keep your speech quite brief – around five minutes is a good average.

Planning your Speech

Preparation is where it all begins, so we open up the many available avenues of research to help you start compiling and building on your speech material. That material needs to be suitable, of course, so make sure that your words don't start a fight or upset granny. We look in detail at what to keep and what to chuck. Remember: if in doubt, leave it out!

Cardinal rules

Unaccustomed as you are, you're scheduled for a spot of speech-making. Stick to the cardinal rules and make your piece a sure-fire success.

Pick the right tone

Tone can be tricky. In making your speech, you have to fulfil certain obligations. You need to express thanks and convey affection. You need to be sincere. You need to entertain. What you don't need to do is come across as dull and pompous – or as a failed stand-up comedian.

A speech without humour is a boring thing indeed, but a speech that sounds like Bernard Manning on an off-night can be impersonal and lacking in warmth. Be funny, but never risk giving offence.

The ideal tone to aim for is one of gentle humour and warmth, intimacy and affection. Aim for something that makes everyone feel included.

Keep it short

However fabulous your speech, the golden rule is always to leave your audience wanting more. Your performance should, as Oscar Wilde once said, 'be exquisite, and leave one unsatisfied.'

Wedding guests enjoy speeches, but don't overestimate their boredom threshold. However funny you are, if you go on too long, noisy coughing fits are sure to set in. With speeches, less is always more and brevity really is the soul of wit. Stick to quick-fire quips rather than shaggy-dog stories; anecdotes rather than twenty-part sagas; pithy comments rather than rambling digressions. To help you get it right, time yourself when you practise.

Don't wing it

Take time to prepare and write your speech. You don't have to scribble everything down at once – keep it on the back burner of your brain for a few weeks before the wedding and jot down ideas as they occur to you.

Ask others for anecdotes and use books and quotations, as well as your imagination, to help you create your masterpiece. Hone your performance by rehearsing, preferably with people you can rely on for honest, constructive feedback.

Include everyone

To make sure no one feels left out, imagine all the different types of people who might be listening to your speech and try to include something for everyone. Avoid in-jokes and make sure you explain references to people and places some listeners may not be familiar with. Be sensitive about the sensibilities of all the guests: that stag-night 'moonie' may not amuse everyone!

Here's a quick checklist to run through a few days before the wedding...

• Does your speech fit the occasion? Is it light-hearted and positive?
• Have you tested it on others and asked for honest feedback?
• Have you timed it to ensure it's not too long?
• Have you been careful not to offend anyone?
  Or leave anyone out?
• Do you know in what order the speeches will be made and at what time?
• If there is a microphone, do you know how to use it?
• Have you written notes, in case you dry up?
• Have you checked names and how to pronounce them?
• Have you made a note of whom you need to thank, or any messages to be read out?

Cardinal sins

Wedding speeches should be memorable. But make sure guests remember your speech for the right reasons – not the fact that you mentioned the bride's three previous husbands. Here's what NOT to do…

Don't mention the war…

Keep in mind that you have a mixed audience. Not everyone will know that Mr Trimble was your woodwork teacher. If an anecdote can't easily be explained, leave it out.

Swear words are a definite no-go area. The last thing you need is granny fainting at a four-letter word.

Bear in mind that causing offence in your wedding speech could be preserved for ever on video, as well as in the minds of the guests and the memories of the couple!

Finally, whatever your feelings about the couple's compatibility, this is not the time to let hostility show. If you can't make a positive speech, delegate to someone who can.

Don't ramble

Being asked to speak is a compliment, so plan properly.
You need to know where you are going with your speech.
You need a definite structure: a beginning, middle and end.

Long, rambling speeches are likely to send the older guests off
to the land of nod, so keep it short. Likewise, long drawn-out
jokes may fall flat if they take too long to tell – spare a thought
for guests' memory lapses.

Don't mumble

The cardinal sins here are swallowing your words, speaking
too fast and losing your place (in which case you might as well
admit it and get a laugh).

This is one of the few times in life when you can be
guaranteed a captive and sympathetic audience. They want
to make life easy for you, so help them. Check early on that
everyone can hear you. Speak slowly and clearly. Signal jokes
by pausing to allow everyone to laugh!

It's their day

Bear in mind that this is the bride and groom's day, not yours. So spare a thought for the couple's blushes – don't mention anything you wouldn't want said about you. Some gentle ribbing about the groom's lack of footballing prowess might be funny. Anecdotes about his lecherous, two-timing ex-girlfriend are almost certainly going too far. If in doubt, leave it out.

Here's a quick recap of those wedding speech no-nos:
NO gags about race, religion or the groom's ex-wife.
NO swearing.
NO private jokes only a few guests will get.
NO ad-libbed off-the-cuff speeches, unless you are very, very good at it!
NO mumbling.
NO gabbling.
NO forgetting the list of people you had to thank or the telegrams you were supposed to read.
NO drinking to excess before you speak.
NO upsetting the bride and groom.

Preparing your speech

Preparation is at the heart of a good speech. Scribbling down a few words the night before the big day is not going to work. Keep your speech on the back burner of your brain as soon as you know you are going to be best man, and start really working on it a few weeks before the wedding.

It's an unfailing rule: the more prepared you are, the more confident you will be about giving your speech, and the more your audience will enjoy it. And the more you'll enjoy it, too.

Putting it all together

Decide what kind of speech you want to make before you start putting it together. You could:

- Make a speech on your own.
- Make a joint speech.
- Perform a stunt and/or use props.
- Use a home video or slides or invent funny telegrams.
- Adopt a well-known format to comic effect.

For examples of sample speeches and more ideas, see the relevant chapters in this book for each speaker.

Break down each element

Don't think about your speech as one big lump. Break it down into headings and decide what you're going to say under each one – for instance, how you met the groom, the wedding preparations, or how the bride and groom got to know each other. Then look at all the elements and work out the best order in which to fit them together.

As you prepare, make sure you have:
• A notebook so you can start jotting down ideas as they occur to you.
• A tape recorder so you can practise and time your speech.
• Friends and family to listen to your speech and give you ideas.
• Any necessary props.
• A copy of the latest draft of your speech to carry round with you, so you can make notes and work on it whenever you have a spare moment.

The following pages will give you a few ideas of where to start and what you could include in your speech.

Revealing sources

Good research can turn a mildly amusing speech into an uproariously funny one. Nothing can beat that cringe-inducing anecdote or photo from the couple's early years that you have managed to excavate and that they were clearly hoping no one could possibly remember – and may even have forgotten about themselves.

You may not know much about their family life or early schooldays – times people enjoy hearing anecdotes about. So start your research early so that you have time to gather everything you need.

Friends united

The best sources of stories about a bride and groom are, of course, their friends and family. Siblings, cousins, mates and colleagues probably all have some great anecdotes to tell. As soon as you know you're doing a speech, send out emails asking people who know the happy couple for any funny/touching stories they think you could include. Or invite everyone out for a drink, bring your tape recorder along and let them reminisce away. You're sure to come away with some great material.

Every picture tells a story

Photograph albums are a great source of speech material, too. Old pictures, or the stories behind them, can be hilarious. If there's a snap of the groom or bride pulling a face in a school photo or looking cute as a toddler, get it blown up to display on the night and work it into the speech.

For instance, a picture of the groom as a five-year-old enjoying a donkey ride at the seaside can be used as an illustration of his lifelong affection for the gee-gees, while a snap of him as a naked tot at bathtime can show how much he's always loved water sports, for example.

Not everyone at the wedding will have known the bride and groom for long. Using photographs of them as tiny children can help to bridge the gap between friends and family. It also gives you licence to comment on their childhood hobbies, eccentricities, fashion sense, etc and make comical comparisons with the grown-up people they are today.

What the papers say

Are there any newspaper cuttings about the happy couple? Perhaps he appeared in the local paper in his days as top goal scorer for the under-nines football team, or she was a prize-winning Girl Guide. You could use this type of material to illustrate how much they've changed… or how much they haven't, as the case may be.

You could also look at the news for the year the groom was born and work it into your speech. For example: '1969 was the year Neil Armstrong took a small step for man and a giant leap for mankind by walking on the moon, and coincidentally, it was also the year Paul took his first steps…'

PCs can be used to great effect to create front page newspaper mock-ups: you could use a Sun headline such as 'Gotcha' to accompany a picture of the couple getting engaged. Get the picture blown up as large as possible and display it while you're making your speech.

Written in the stars

Zodiac signs make for great speech fodder. Use them to compare the characteristics/vices of the sign the bride/groom were born under to the way they actually are. If, for instance, the groom's star sign says he's generous and brave, but in fact he's notoriously thrifty and a bit of a coward, you're well away.

For example: 'Geminis are meant to be communicative and witty, with a reputation for being the life and soul of the party. Well, I guess that's one way of describing James on his stag night...' Or: 'Richard's such a quiet, gentle guy that many people don't realize he's a Leo, which is, of course, a fire sign. But I can assure you that, as far as Helen is concerned, he's burning up with passion.'

Books that discuss star sign compatibility can also provide some funny lines for speeches, as can reading out the horoscope for the day. It doesn't need to be a real one – just make up something to suit the occasion, for example: 'My horoscope says today is a day for pure relaxation – wonder what went wrong there then?'

By any other name...

There's often mileage in the meaning of the names of the bride or groom: 'Apparently, the name Gary means "spear carrier". Well, I don't know about a spear but he certainly carries a torch for Kathleen.' You could also compare the meanings of the couple's names.

Stars in their eyes

Think of a famous person with whom the bride or groom shares a name and compare them in terms of image, job, clothes, etc. For example, 'Tom Cruise may have made his millions and worked with most of Hollywood's major directors, while our Tom has made a few quid and enjoys a pint of Directors. However, I think he's the more fortunate guy, as Tom Cruise didn't have much luck with Nicole, but our Tom has got Isabel, and their love is something money and fame can't buy.'

Whatever they like...

You don't have to stick to jokes about football teams –
hobbies and interests of all kinds can form the basis of lots of
stories. However, you might not be as familiar with the
groom's obsessions as he is. In this case, the internet is a great
source of information.

If one of the happy couple is a huge fan of any singer or
celebrity and their obsession is well known, you could use it
in your speech. For example: 'Roger has always been a major
Elvis fan, and when he met Rachel he was certainly All Shook
Up. He almost moved into Heartbreak Hotel when he thought
she wasn't interested...'

Make it work

Working life and old bosses can be a source of great material.
If you're not a colleague of the bride or groom, get in touch
with their workmates past and present and ask them for any
good office anecdotes. Just make sure they're not too in-jokey
so that everyone will understand them.

Ha ha ha

Jokes, jokes, jokes – everyone like to hear them at weddings. As well as your own jokes, renting comedy videos and films, asking people for their favourite gags and looking for funny lines on the internet can also provide you with inspiration.

If you do borrow jokes, you will need to personalize them to make them appropriate, rather than just throw them into the speech. The following sections of this book are full of examples of how to do this. Go for quality rather than quantity: a handful of well-polished witticisms will do you better service than a scatter-gun approach involving a hundred ill-digested one-liners.

Academic archive

Old schoolbooks, school reports and university notes can also provide material. Ask one of the family to get them down from the attic and take a look. If there's a school report saying how your high-flying friend will never amount to a hill of beans, or a funny essay they wrote when they were ten, it could be amusing to read it out.

Hands-on help

If you're worried about any aspect of your speech, talk it through with someone who's been there before. Talking to someone with experience will calm your nerves and give your confidence a boost. They survived the ordeal, after all! And if they still have a copy of their speech, ask to see it. They can also advise on how to source material, where they got their ideas from and how they put the whole thing together.

You can also learn from their mistakes, rather than making your own. They may have unwittingly stumbled on a sensitive subject, for example, or their speech may have overrun or been too short. Ask them which were the bits that really worked, and what were the things that could, in retrospect, have been improved on. Finding out how not to do it can be a great help in making your own effort a success. And if they are willing, ask them to read your speech after you've written it, for some last-minute expert advice.

The right material

Wedding speakers have it tough. Who else has to make a speech that will appeal to an audience with an age range of 2 to 82? Speeches have to make people laugh without offending anyone's sensibilities, talk about families and relationships without treading on anyone's toes and hold people's attention without stealing the show from the happy couple.

It sounds like a tall order, but most of the pitfalls of speech-making can be avoided if you know what to talk about and recognize that there are limits around certain subjects. It's all a matter of choosing and using your material with care.

Definite no-nos

You can get away with talking about a lot of subjects, provided you're genuinely witty and don't cross the line into bad taste. Some things, however, are absolutely off-limits. Steer clear of these topics:

- Race
- Religion
- Ex-partners
- People who refused to attend
- Last-minute threats to call off the wedding
- Swearing
- Explicit sexual references

Criticism

Weddings aren't the place for criticism. Don't knock anything relating to the venue or the service, and don't make jokes at other people's expense, especially the bride's. This is the happy couple's perfect day, and you need to help keep it that way by considering other people's feelings at all times.

Past romances

There's nothing wrong with talking about the groom's previous loves – provided they're really firmly in the far distant past.

Tell guests about the flirtation he had with that cute little blonde… in the sandpit back at nursery school.

Don't tell them about the girl who broke his heart when he was 16 and whom he's never really forgotten – or about any other romance he's had since the age of seven, for that matter. It's also worth noting that while you can make vague allusions to the groom's sowing of wild oats – such as 'He was a bit of a wild lad at college' – you should never even hint at anything similar about the bride. Double standards still apply, at least at weddings!

The happy couple's relationship

Comments about the bride and groom are usually part of every wedding speech. Tread carefully, however, especially if their relationship has been stormy in the past.

Tell guests about how their first meeting generated enough electricity to power the National Grid. Talk about how compatible they are and how great they both look today.

Don't tell them about how they slept together within half-an-hour of meeting or about how she left him for someone else for six months. Arguments, estrangements and threats to call off the wedding are all off limits. If in any doubt, leave it out.

Bit of a lad

People expect funny stories about the groom's misdemeanours, especially when part of the best man's speech. Joshing him gently is all part of the fun, but do make sure that your anecdotes are humorous rather than offensive.

Tell guests about the time he redecorated the living room with crayon when he was a little lad.

Don't tell them about how he was all over that lap dancer at his stag night, then vomited copiously in the minicab all the way home. Keep quiet about criminal records, expulsions from school and the like, too.

Family matters

Complimenting the bride and groom's families can be part of your speech – but make sure you stick to compliments only. **Tell guests** how the bride/groom have great parents – and now they're gaining great parents-in-law, as well as a lovely wife/husband. Or congratulate the parents for organizing the wedding so well.

Don't tell them how you're amazed to see the bride/groom's father there at all since he scarpered when the groom was still in his pram. Speeches shouldn't be used for settling scores. Avoid comments about divorced or warring parents. If the family situation is very sensitive, resist the temptation to think you can make things better with a few carefully chosen lines.

The bride

It's possible that you may have ambivalent feelings about the bride. Keep these firmly under wraps at the wedding. Don't make any jokey remarks about her diet either! Compliments to the bride are the only permissible references to her in your speech.

Be kind

Remember, if you're opting for a funny speech to mix the mockery with some sincerity. Talk about how highly you think of both the bride and groom and how their relationship together has enriched each other. Give the couple all your very best wishes for the future.

The wedding

Behind-the-scenes stories about preparing for the wedding, especially amusing incidents and narrowly averted disasters, make good ingredients for speeches. However, you might be surprised at how sensitive these subjects can be. No family exists who doesn't squabble over wedding arrangements. Sometimes these disagreements seem amusing by the time the big day arrives – but sometimes they don't, so take care.

Tell guests how fantastically the day has turned out and how it's all down to the hard work of all the organizers.

Don't tell them about how the bride's mother almost had a nervous breakdown over the seating plan – unless you're absolutely sure she'll think it's funny. As always, run your speech by someone close to the family first.

In-jokes

Making everyone feel included is an important job of any speaker. To make sure no one feels left out, think of all the people who might be listening when you write your speech.

You need to explain references that not everyone may be familiar with, and if this takes too long, it's better to think of another anecdote.

Tell guests about how, one year, the bride/groom broke three dozen eggs in the school egg and spoon race.

Don't tell them about that hilarious time in design and technology class when the bride/groom got told off by that mad Mr Smith, you know, the technology teacher, he was really mad, and he sent her/him to see Miss Green, the one who all the lads fancied... you really had to be there.

Tailored to fit

The material that you decide is suitable for your speech will depend on your audience. It's up to you to find out who you'll be talking to, and to check beforehand that what you want to say won't cause offence. If you can rehearse your speech in front of your mum and granny without them feeling uncomfortable or you feeling embarrassed, you're probably on to a winner.

Delivery

It ain't what you do...

As anyone who's made a successful speech will tell you, it's not what you say, it's the way you say it. And, you want to make sure the way you deliver and present your speech does justice to your carefully written speech. Here's how.

Practice makes perfect

Reading your speech out again and again before the big day is essential if you want to perfect your delivery, make sure your material is suitable – and find out if your jokes are funny. Your speech should appeal to everyone, from your friends to your maiden aunt, so try to rehearse in front of a variety of people. Test it out on people who will give honest, constructive feedback. They will also be able to tell you when you're mumbling, or rambling, or just going on too long. You should also record your rehearsals on tape. That way, you will be able to review yourself and see where there's room for improvement and how you are for time – aim for five minutes as a rough guide.

The run-up

You've enjoyed a tearful moment during the wedding ceremony and the celebrations and reception have begun. Good food and wine is flowing but all you can think about is how nervous you are about your imminent speech. How you fill your time will affect your delivery...

Don't overindulge

Although it's very tempting to down a few too many glasses while you're waiting to speak – don't. Being tipsy could affect your delivery by making you slur your words and cause you to be unsteady on your feet. Too many drinks might also lead you to decide that the risqué story which you deleted from your original speech, really should be in there after all.

Have a banana

Many professional performers swear by the trick of eating a banana about 20 minutes before they start speaking. Doing this, they say, will give you a quick energy boost and help steady your nerves.

You're on!

Start right

Don't try to begin your speech when there are lots of distractions. Wait until the audience have your attention or have stopped applauding the previous speaker, the tables have been cleared, the coffee poured and everyone has settled so that you have people's undivided attention.

Rambling prohibited

Timing is crucial when it comes to speeches. However brilliant yours is, and however good a speaker you are, five minutes is more than enough. People enjoy listening to speeches, true, but they want to get on with talking and dancing, too, so keep it short. Rambling speeches are a mistake. Make sure yours has a firm beginning, middle and end. Steer clear of shaggy dog stories in favour of short, pithy jokes and asides. When it comes to speeches, less is definitely more.

Eye to eye

Make eye contact when you're making your speech – just not with everyone at once! Speak as if you were talking to one person and focus on them. You can look around the room if you want to, but focus on one person at a time. The trick is to imagine that you're simply chatting to someone.

Don't look down

Even if you decide to learn your speech off by heart, you
will need to have some notes to refer to in case your mind
goes blank in the heat of the moment. However, don't deliver
your speech while hiding behind a quivering piece of paper
or constantly staring downwards. Look down for a moment,
look up and speak. Get into a rhythm of doing this throughout
your speech.

No mumbling

When people get nervous, they tend to swallow their words;
this can render a beautifully written speech nearly inaudible.
You don't want to deliver your speech only to find that no
one could actually hear what you were saying, so check that
you're audible by arranging beforehand for someone at the
back of the room to signal when your voice isn't carrying.

Breathtaking

Another way to combat the mumbling menace is by breathing
properly. Take deep, rhythmic breaths. This will pump oxygen
into your blood and keep your brain sharp and alert.

Set the pace

Gabbling is another thing people tend to do when they're nervous. To stop yourself talking too fast, write the word 'pause' at intervals through your notes, or if you are using cue cards, insert blank ones that will automatically cause you to slow down. If you do lose your place, it's best just to make a joke of it.

Move on swiftly

Pause briefly after you make a joke to give people a chance to laugh, but keep jokes and anecdotes short so that if one doesn't work, you can move on quickly to the next. If your joke dies, don't despair. Turn the situation to your advantage by inserting a quip such as 'Only me on that one then', or look round at an imaginary assistant and say: 'Start the car!' 'Rescue lines' like these can earn you a chuckle from a momentarily awkward silence.

Keep smiling

Making a speech is supposed to be fun, so make sure you don't look utterly miserable when you're doing it. Smile! Think of something that makes you laugh before you start speaking to get yourself into the fun mood. Body language is important, too, so adopt a relaxed posture before you begin – no crossed arms or fidgeting.

Stage fright

It's only natural to be nervous. If you find that you're really scared when you begin, don't panic. Make a joke out of it instead. Lines like 'This speech is brought to you in association with Imodium' or 'I was intending to speak but my tongue seems to be welded to the roof of my mouth' should raise a laugh and will help to get the audience on your side. One completely bald father of the bride started off on a high note by remarking: 'As you can see, I've been so worried about making this speech, I've been tearing my hair out.' There's no shame in admitting you're a wee bit scared.

Start strongly

Opening lines are important, because they grab the audience's attention and get you off to a good start. Something like: 'Ladies and gentlemen, they say speeches are meant to be short and sweet, so thank you and good night,' should help you to begin in style.

All in the mind

Instead of seeing your speech as a formal ordeal, think of it as being a conversation between you and a lot of people you know and really like, or as a way of wishing two good friends well. Thinking positively about your speech and the reason why you are there will help you to deliver it with confidence and make the task seem less intimidating.

To help calm your nerves beforehand, imagine your speech being over and everyone applauding. Imagine how you'll feel when you can sit down and relax, knowing that the moment is over and you can now really enjoy the rest of the evening. By visualizing everything going well, you should gain even more confidence.

They're on your side

Remember that weddings are happy occasions and all the guests want to see everything go well, including your speech. Be assured, the audience is on your side, they're all rooting for you, so make the most of it and use their goodwill to boost your confidence.

Give it meaning

Think about the meaning of your speech while you're making it. Concentrate on the thoughts you want to convey and the message behind your words, rather than just reciting your notes, as this will help you to make your delivery more expressive.

Round it off

End your speech with a toast. This will give it a focus and provide something to work towards. After you make your toast, you can sit down when everyone else sits down, signifying a definite end to your speech.

Our range of sample toasts starts on page 162.

Using prompts and props

Memory joggers

Reading an entire speech from a sheet of paper can make it sound a bit lifeless and can stop you from making eye contact with the audience. One way to get around this is to memorize your speech and use prompts to remind you of what to say.

To cut down on the amount of text you use, first write the speech out, then make very brief notes that remind you of each part of it. Gradually cut back on your text, so the notes say as much as you need to jog your memory.

On cue

Make a set of cue cards. These are small index cards with key phrases that remind you of different parts of your speech, stacked in the order that you say them. Inserting blank cards for pauses can help you pace your speech. Even if you feel you need to put your whole speech on cards, they are still preferable to a piece of paper, because you will need to pause and look up as you turn them.

Proper props

Physical gags, games, visuals and tricks can all be part of a good speech. So if you don't want to be stuck just reading a prepared text – don't be. Let your imagination run wild.

If your speech is going to involve the use of props, make sure that you do plenty of rehearsing with them beforehand, and also ensure that any machinery is in good working order before the big day.

Make 'em look

Simple props can be used to begin with a bang. One best man, for instance, started off his speech with the remark: 'I hate it when people use cheap gimmicks to get attention, don't you?' before whipping off his baseball cap and pony tail to reveal a completely bald pate.

Lots of different props can be used for this type of joke. Why not try:
• A revolving bow tie
• Clown feet
• A whistle
• A clown nose?

Great gags

Little trike

One motorcycle-mad groom thought he'd do something really different on his wedding day by roaring into the reception on his brand-new Harley Davidson. Only, unknown to him, his younger brother-cum-best man had got wind of the plan. As the groom arrived at the top table on his gleaming steed, he heard a strange creaking noise coming from the back of the room. He turned around to see his brother upstage him completely by trailing behind on a child's rusty tricycle.

Mopping up

Harry and Jane are a couple both known for their sensitivity, so when they got married it wasn't surprising that both Harry and bride Jane were in floods of tears before the speeches had even started. But when the time came for Harry's speech, Jane decided to be prepared. Before beginning his speech, she produced an enormous plastic bag stuffed with packets of tissues, which she distributed among the audience. It wasn't long before they were throwing them at him.

Loud and clear

A quick visual gag can get a speech off to a great start,
as Michael demonstrated when he was father of the bride.
When he started speaking the audience couldn't hear a word
because he was mumbling so much – until he produced
a huge loudhailer and roared 'Can you hear me at the
back?' through it.

Picture perfect

When he was best man for his friend Pete, Richard decided to
use a flip chart of photographs and a pointer to liven up his
speech. Only the pictures weren't ones of the happy couple as
toddlers or newspaper cuttings of their achievements. Instead
there was a skip – representing Pete's first car; a picture of a
bombsite – representing his bedroom; and so on. It was a
simple idea, but it got big laughs.

Read the signs

Introduce your speech by saying that you've got a sore throat and can't speak very loudly, so your friend is going to use sign language to interpret what you're saying. Your friend will then make exaggerated and ridiculous hand gestures to accompany your speech. Obviously, this one will need a lot of rehearsal.

Hat trick

Have a series of funny hats under the table that you put on as you run through the groom's life story – for example a baby bonnet, a school cap, a mortar board, a fireman's helmet, a baseball cap, a deerstalker. The more ridiculous the hats, the better.

Good report

Write a mock school report on the bride or groom and read it out, relating it to the events of the day, such as: 'It says here that Paula doesn't suffer fools gladly... which is bad news as she's just got married to Steve.'

Video diary

Get your friends together and make a spoof video documentary featuring their thoughts and feelings about the bride and groom. A couple could dress up as the happy couple and re-enact their first meeting.

Games to play

Playing speech games is a way of getting the whole audience to join in the fun. Try:

The singing game

Ask friends and family to help compile a list of words that describe the guests at each table. Put the lists on the respective tables and ask everyone sitting at them to make up a song or poem using all of the words on the list. They then have to stand up and perform it!

The limerick game

This is another word game that everyone can enjoy. You put a note on all the tables asking the guests to make up a short poem or limerick about the couple. You can read out the best ones during your speech, or ask the guests to read out their own. Make it clear however, that you don't want anything offensive.

The sweepstake game

At the start of the reception, get the ushers to ask guests to bet on the length of the speeches. The person who makes the closest guess wins the total amount, either to keep or to donate to a charity of their choice.

The key game

This is a favourite among wedding speechmakers as it really helps to break the ice. To play it, you need to get in touch with all the female guests beforehand (you might have to hang around the ladies at the reception to do it) and fill them in on the plan.

During your speech you then say something like: 'Neil has got what you might call a chequered past, but now that he's married to Hannah it's time that he began afresh. So I'm asking any of his ex-girlfriends who may be present to give back the keys to his flat. Just come up here and put them in this bowl. Come on girls, don't be shy.'

Then, you've guessed it, all the women at the reception, from the groom's 90-year-old auntie to his four-year-old cousin will come up to put a set of keys in the bowl. It's guaranteed to get laughs and helps everyone to relax.

Instant nostalgia

Props don't have to be used for jokes. You could put together a spoof video documentary with friends and family being interviewed on what a great couple they make, or compile photographs and newspaper cuttings to make a quick 'this is your life' of the bride and groom. Or, why not have a blast from the past by playing a tape of the band the groom used to be in or an old video of the bride as a child performing in the nativity play at school.

As with speeches, so with props. You should never attempt to wing it when making a speech, but this is even more important to remember when using props. Make sure that you rehearse well and run your idea by other members of the wedding party to reduce the risk of your joke falling flat.

How to be funny

Make 'em laugh!

Every speaker wants to raise the roof – or at least a few smiles. Don't feel under pressure to be funny. Remember that everyone's on your side and they want your words to work as much as you do.

- Establish a rapport with your audience by referring to something topical that all present can relate to: 'Phew! I don't know about you but I thought I was going to keel over in that church…'
- Nervous? Don't panic. Make a gag about Imodium or jelly legs!
- Try and enjoy yourself – or look like you are. It'll relax the room.
- Keep it simple. If you have to explain the gag, you're doing it wrong!
- Practice makes perfect. Test out your speech on friends and colleagues, note their reactions and amend as necessary.
- Think of your whole audience. Avoid private in-jokes, technical jargon and anything that might offend granny.
- Be sensitive. Avoid referring to previous partners, weight problems etc, but if you have to, do so with great care. Above all, don't offend the bride. If in doubt, leave it out!
- Be brief. Even the best speech can become a yawn if it goes on too long.
- Jokes aren't everything. Sometimes a few words spoken from the heart can be just as effective.

Timing and delivery

You know what they say: 'The secret of comedy... is... in... the... timing.' And then they say: 'It ain't what you say, it's the way that you say it.' Well, they may be clichés, but they're no less true for all that. Check out these tips:

- Speak clearly. It doesn't matter how great your material is if no one can make out what you're saying.
- Always keep the punchline a surprise. If the end of your joke is 'Five donkeys and a unicorn', make sure you don't mention the keywords 'donkeys' or 'unicorn' in the build-up.
- Take a good long breath between each sentence. Public speakers invariably speed up as they go, and what to you sounds nice and slow may well come over at breakneck speed.
- If you can, check out the venue beforehand. Get someone to stand at the back and make sure that you can be heard.
- If people are laughing, enjoy the ride! Don't try and talk over them.
- Check out any props and equipment you're planning on using. Have an emergency fall-back plan: what will you do if the slide projector/microphone breaks down?
- Treat wedding hecklers with a smile. They're usually good-natured.

What the experts say

'The more you practise delivering your speech, the less nervous you will be. Practise the pauses, the intonations, the anecdotes. By showing you've put even a little thought and effort into what you're saying, all manner of sins will be forgiven. Recite your speech in the shower. On the bus. On the loo. On the night, your nerves will thank you, because instead of fretting about the audience or your flies, you'll simply focus on what you're going to say.'
Rob Pointer, stand-up comic and serial best man

'Don't speak when you're looking down at your notes. Look down for a moment, look up, smile at everyone, speak – then repeat. You don't need to talk constantly; it gives guests a break, and if you're not afraid of silence, you'll look confident, so everyone can relax. Remember that in between speaking, silence feels approximately ten times longer than it is, so take it nice and slow.'
Jill Edwards, comedy coach and scriptwriter

Lines that work – and lines that don't...

Always a winner

'Not for the first time today do I rise from a warm seat clutching a piece of paper...'

'I'm going to make this short and sweet. Thanks very much.' [Speaker sits down.]

'And so without further ado, let's raise our glasses...'

'I'm sure you'll agree that I'm the luckiest man/woman in the world today.'

'I do!'

Definite no-nos

'I wouldn't say the bride looks fat in that dress, but...'

'Turning now to Simon's third marriage...'

'Not being a big fan of marriage myself...'

'When I was going out with the bride/groom...'

'Frankly, I'm amazed we've got this far without my parents coming to blows...'

Any reference to bridal pregnancy (except by prior agreement).

References to the cost of the wedding.

Good for a groan

'Unaccustomed as I am to public speaking...'

'My wife/husband and I...'

Wedding speech checklist

Once you've agreed to speak

No matter how much warning you've had of your role on the big day, the success of your speech will ultimately depend on the amount of prep you've put in. So as soon as you accept the job…

- Start thinking about research.
- Think about the audience. Your speech will have to appeal to a wide range of people, from great aunt Nora to your friends from work.
- It's your job to find out who'll be among the guests so that your material appeals and you don't cause offence.
- Ask friends and family for funny stories/embarrassing pictures that you can build into your speech.
- Keep your speech in the back of your mind. You never know when you might pick up a titbit of information or some juicy material.
- Keep a notebook to hand. Great ideas often strike when you least expect them (like on the train or in the bath!).
- Speak to someone who's been a wedding speaker before and find out what not to do.
- Decide on the kind of speech you want. Will you need any props or visual aids or any equipment?

The build-up

A few weeks before the big day, start working on your speech in earnest.

- Think about the structure. Would the speech be better broken down into manageable chunks/themes?
- Does your speech do what it's supposed to do? Is it funny, affectionate and charming without being offensive?
- Have you included everything you need to in your speech?
- Gather all the props/presentation aids you'll need and make sure you know how to use them.
- Build in time to practise your speech – the better rehearsed you are, the more confident you'll be, and the more everyone will enjoy it, yourself included.

Only a week to go

A week or so before the big day, start honing down
your speech.

- Use a tape recorder or video to record yourself.
- Rope in an audience of friends to practise on.
- Be sure to practise your speech with any props you plan
  to use – winging it on the day is not a good bet.
- Time your speech. Aim to keep it to around five minutes.
  Brevity really is the soul of wit.
- Don't forget to allow time for reading out messages
  from absent friends and family, passing on practical
  announcements and so on.
- Write your speech in note form on cue cards, even if you
  intend to commit it to memory.
- Think positively about your speech and it will feel like less
  of an ordeal.
- Visualize your speech being over and everyone applauding
  as it will help to give you confidence and calm your nerves.
- Remember the audience is on your side – you'll be able to
  use their goodwill to boost your confidence.

The big day

A few last pointers to help your speech go smoothly:

- Try to relax and take it easy.
- Try not to look for Dutch courage in the bottom of your wineglass – you'll do your speech more harm than good!
- Keep busy with your other duties; this will help you to focus, and keep away those pre-speech nerves.
- Have your notes with you, even if you've committed your speech to memory. If your mind goes blank or you feel yourself veering off the point, at least you can refer to them, to get back on track.
- End your speech with a toast – it will give you something to work towards and be a clear signal that your bit is over.

20 top tips

So, you've read all the advice and got some idea of how you might start to tackle writing your wedding speech. Here's a recap of the most important top tips to remember…

Take note
As soon as you know that you'll be making a speech at the wedding – this is usually some time in advance – get into the habit of carrying a notebook around with you so you can jot down any thoughts or memories that could be worked into your speech. The best ideas often come to you at the most unlikely moments…

Structure your speech
Don't try writing it all in one go! Break down your words into the different areas you want to cover, such as thanking the guests, stories about the run-up to the wedding, anecdotes about the groom, words for the bride and your speech's conclusion. Take the jottings from your notebook and see where they fit into the plan.

Get sorted – in triplicate
Anxiety about losing the text of your speech can ruin a whole wedding morning. Make three or four copies of the final version and give each one to a different guest to look after. It's impossible for all the copies to be lost – and it will put your mind at rest!

Make eye contact

... but not with everyone at once! Speak as if you were talking to one person, and address them directly. Of course you will want to look around the room, but take time to focus on one person at a time.

Everyone's rooting for you!

It's true. This is a wedding and, although the scale of the occasion might initially seem daunting, it is in many ways the easiest public speaking opportunity of all. Everyone is on your side and no one wants you to do badly.

Practise – on tape

Reading your speech out again and again – preferably to other people – is essential when you're practising. Making a recording of yourself can be useful, too. Listen out for places where you speak too fast or where the point you're making is unclear, and revise your speech accordingly.

Speak to both sides

Make sure your speech will mean something to everyone present. There may be guests who know only half of the wedding party (if that), and they may not even know you. In-jokes and favourite anecdotes should be told in such a way that everyone can enjoy them, so explain any esoteric references as you go.

Don't rely on memory

You may have practised your speech so hard that you're sure you know it by heart. Keep your text handy anyway – the stress of public speaking can sometimes cause people to forget their lines.

Be brief

Brevity truly is the soul of wit. Some speakers plan optional sections that can be cut if the speech isn't going too well. At any rate, you should time your speech and stick to it – five minutes is perfectly long enough.

But they didn't laugh...

Keep jokes and anecdotes short, so that if one doesn't work, you can swiftly move on to the next. And don't laugh at your own jokes – you'll soon know whether you've scored a hit!

Get your stories straight

Often a bride and groom may have a story in their past that lends itself to a good anecdote. But if the story is at all well known, check with the other speakers just to make sure that your material doesn't duplicate anyone else's.

Language barrier

Although to you your speech is something written, to your guests it is something spoken. So make sure your language is not too stiff or formal. Change all the 'could nots' to 'couldn'ts', and make free with the first person.

It's not a speech...

In most people's minds, the word 'speech' is associated with great tension, formality and the need to perform well. But thinking of it instead as part of a conversation at a largish dinner party, or simply as a few words to wish some friends well, will make the whole thing seem less intimidating.

Playing the waiting game

Actually sitting and waiting for your moment to come is probably more stressful than the speaking itself. Once you're up and away, the momentum of the speech takes over and you'll start to relax once you hear a laugh or two. So, while you're waiting, repeat your first line to yourself. It also helps if you can get involved in the other speeches – really make a point of listening and responding to them. It'll be your turn before you know it.

It's your call

There are traditions and customs about who should speak and what they should say but, if it suits you, feel free to ignore any or all of them. Give the speech on your own terms and you'll achieve the best result. So, if you want to give only a brief toast rather than a long spiel, fine. If you're the best man and you don't feel like humiliating the groom, that's fine, too. It's entirely up to you.

Breathing space

When speaking or reading in public, people have a marked tendency to rush their words without realizing it. So, it's a good idea to insert the word 'pause' at intervals in your speech or, if you're using cue cards, to insert blank cards that will automatically slow you down.

Doing the introductions

If you have a toastmaster, he or she should take care of introducing each speaker. Otherwise, this is the best man's job. Make sure that each speaker is introduced by name and position before they start – this will stop guests talking among themselves as they try to work out who's speaking.

Not now...

Whenever the speeches are scheduled to take place – at the end of the meal is the norm – make sure that nothing else is going on and that all the clearing up has stopped. Speakers need everyone's undivided attention!

Preparing the speech

When writing your speech, always bear in mind at what point your speech comes in the order of play. Will you need to cover certain subjects? Will you be speaking on behalf of anyone? Will you be expected to address certain themes? Will you need to reply to another speaker/toast? These considerations should help you plan your words.

Full stop

However silly or serious your speech may be, it's always a good idea to end it with a toast. For you it's something to work towards, and for the guests it's an immediately recognizable punctuation point.

Winning Lines

A good speech has a strong beginning, a meaty middle and ends on a high. That's why we've included this section on beginnings, middles and endings.

Simply read it through, select the sections that appeal and copy them in order. That way you've got a basic structure to work with.

Strong starts

Introduction

If you don't start strongly, guests will glaze over until the champagne toast. Try these to get you going...

Opening gambits

'I'm here to sing Paul's/Louise's praises. You'll be glad to hear, though, that I can't sing and there isn't much to praise, so fortunately this speech should be short and sweet.'

'Excuse me, but I'm a little nervous. Now I know what a Rowntree's jelly feels like.'

'Did anyone see that polar bear walk by just now? No? Shame, because they're such terrific ice-breakers.'

'They say good speeches are meant to be pithy, although what oranges have got to do with it, I don't know.'

'They say good speeches are meant to be short and sweet... So thanks very much for your time.'

'Ladies and gentlemen, thank you for your kind applause. Not for the first time today do I rise from a warm seat with a piece of paper in my hand...'

One-liners

'The groom was not always as handsome as this. When he was born the midwife took one look and slapped his father. He had the only pram in Bristol with shutters. In fact, he was so ugly his mum used to feed him with a catapult.'

'Jon has a face that launched a thousand ships. And a figure that ate a thousand chips.'

'Greg was always considered a handsome chap at college. He was fastidious about getting his beauty sleep – about 20 hours a day, usually.'

'Tony always used to take Janine out to dine in a secluded corner, lit only by candles. Partly because he's a romantic, but partly because he didn't want to scare her off!'

'Now he's married, Dom can really let himself go… oh, you already have!'

Anecdotes

'The first time Bill and Emily went away together, Emily wanted Bill to act as if they were married, to avoid any disapproving looks. So Bill let her carry the suitcases.'

'Was it love at first sight the night Ian and Sue met? There are several theories about this. Sue contends that it was love at first sight, but then she found out he already had a boyfriend, so she went home with Ian instead…'

'These two eventually found each other after years of trying. And, as practice makes perfect, they really must be the perfect couple.'

'Rob and I have been great mates for a long time now, and inevitably we've shared many things over the years: our AA counsellor; our probation officer; our therapist; our mums' recipes for bread sauce – and now, a top table. Who'd have thought it?'

Stunts

Prepare a slide show of photographs from the bride/groom's past. Drop your cards as the slide show starts and apologize, saying that they may be in the wrong order. Without looking at the pictures, give a running commentary. For example, accompany a photo of the groom in his primary school uniform with the comment: 'Rob's first day in his new job was a proud moment for the family...'

Write a mock school report for the groom/bride, referring to their character/behaviour at school, and relate this to today. For example, 'It says here that Louise "has a short attention span and responds poorly to authority". Which could be a problem, being married to Damian...'

Pretend to have a copy of the bride or groom's CV and pick out examples of their 'achievements'.

The best man can hold up a box marked Honeymoon Survival Kit, and pull out some props: a tube of Deep Heat; bandages; Spiderman mask; Chelsea shirt; Viagra...

Set pieces

The best man gives a huge parcel to the bride. As she unwraps it, it becomes smaller and smaller. The parcel, in fact, contains nothing but a note saying, 'Thanks for padding my speech out for me, I've got nothing at all to say...'

Organize a sweepstake on the length of your speech. Keep asking the timekeeper how long you've taken and then – at apparently the most important part of the speech – abruptly sit down and announce that you've won.

The best man, or father of the bride, introduces a song, poem or tribute to the bride or groom from a football team or drama group or club of which they are a member.

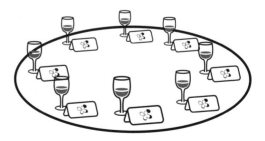

Meaty middles

Aim to add between three and six 'fillings' to your speech sandwich. Such as…

Aaaah…

Something sentimental, without being too gushy, can be a nice touch…

'To have joy one must share it. Happiness was born a twin.' (Lord Byron)

'Absence diminishes little passions and increases great ones, just as the wind blows out a candle and fans a fire.' (La Rochefoucauld)

'Do not be afraid to love these days. Take them gently and with a consideration for eternity, but take them as your own. Have patience with your dreams and the expectations that you have, but do not defer all hope to the future for there are only so many tomorrows.' (Brian Baron)

'Keep your minds set on the future, your memories planted in the past, and always your hearts where they are right at this moment.' (Anon)

'Hold on to yesterday, but not too tightly; let loose just enough to reach tomorrow.' (Anon)

Religious references

'Thankfully our hosts, unlike those at the wedding feast at Canae, haven't insisted on saving the best wine till last! Though looking at one or two of you here today, I'm not sure you'd notice…'

'In the words of Saint Paul: "Forgive each other as soon as a quarrel begins." Which is God's way of saying never go to sleep on an argument…'

'As the Bible says: "Who so findeth a wife, findeth a good thing." Now when I look at Jane, I can't help thinking, what a complete understatement!'

'When God created man and woman in his own image, we're told he blessed them and said: "Be fruitful and multiply…" Now whatever did He mean by that?'

'Saint Paul advises us that "a husband must love his wife as he loves himself". Now if Jerry can pull THAT off, then Penny'll be a really lucky gal…'

Jokes

'Sam and Sally are like very different wines: Sam gets better with age, whereas Sally just gets drunk.'

'Bob used to do 40 push-ups every morning to make sure he could keep up with Kirsty. Now he needs 40 winks…'

'Paula is busy making their new home comfortable, although Mark told me he's quite happy with his chair in the King's Head.'

'There are three kinds of wedding ring: the engagement ring, the wedding ring and the suffer-ring!'

'How many bridesmaids does it take to change a light bulb? Five. One to yank it out of the socket and chuck it, and four to squabble over who's going to catch it.'

Observations

'Some say that star-sign compatibility is the secret of a happy marriage. But I don't really believe in all that stuff – which is unusual for a Scorpio…'

'Some (single) people think that marriage will limit them or hold them back. But look at James and Katie today, and you see two people whose lives have expanded and flourished in every way since they got together…'

'My gran, who's been married 50 years, says the secret of a successful marriage is give and take. I said: "You mean 50:50"? She said: "NO! You've both got to give 110 per cent!"'

Quips

'Confucius, I believe, said something very significant about the meaning of marriage. But it was in Chinese, so I'm afraid I didn't understand it.'

"Thanks for giving me away Dad," Sally said to me this morning. "Think nothing of it," I replied. "I've been trying to do it for years!"'

'Given that Jemima and I have been living together for eight years, I thought that for once we deserved to walk up an aisle that's not located in Sainsbury's.'

Asides

These are useful little remarks to allow you to comment on something topical or specific to the big day.

'Before I continue, has anyone ever been to a wedding this posh before? Even the cockroaches have got place names…'

'Today was already shaping up to be a wonderful occasion – but look outside and you'll agree that, with gorgeous sunshine in mid-November, we've been truly blessed.'

[Note handed to speaker by usher]
'And before we go any further, some important news just in: Rochdale 4, Hartlepool 2.'

'By the way, please don't worry if you hear any unusual noises during the speeches – it's only Jim's wallet groaning in agony…'

'I must say I'm surprised by today's downpour. Sarah's parents have been such terrific wedding organizers, I assumed they'd be able to control the weather too!'

On this occasion...

'It's amazing, really, that Rob ever got as far as the wedding reception. He's a terrible driver and he's never got change for the bus.'

'This occasion is rather like a football game: two raucous tribes, soused to the gills, gathered together to witness a cracking match...'

'Having had the pleasure of getting to know both families here today, I can see that this occasion is going to be a great opportunity for two wonderful sets of people to meet and mingle.'

'A wedding is a wonderful opportunity for people to make new friends and form relationships. So as chief bridesmaid can I just say: "Bagsy first dance with the best man!"'

'This occasion reminds me of my own wedding, all those years ago. And what a close-run thing that was!'

End on a high!

Nobody wants your speech to end. So leave them wanting more with something like…

'I'd like to thank you for your patience and kind attention, and to those of you who managed to stay awake: cheers!'

'That's all from me, except to say that, for those of you who've never given a speech at a wedding before, if you get an audience half as generous as you lot, you'll enjoy every minute of it…'

'So, without further ado, I'd like you charge your glasses and thank the Almighty that I'm finally going to sit down and shut up. Cheers!'

'To the happy couple, may their happiness be complete, their marriage long and prosperous and every wedding speech they hear be funnier and shorter than mine…'

'And, in the words of that world-famous orator, Bugs Bunny: "That's all, folks!"'

Final thoughts

'One final thought. If marriage is a two-way street, how come my wife keeps telling me that it's "my way or the highway"?'

'One final thought. Always listen carefully to your partner's advice, so that when things go wrong you can say "I told you so"!'

'And finally, marriage should be like supporting a football team: sometimes happy, sometimes sad, but always exciting for about an hour and a half on a Saturday!

'Don't forget. Never put off until tomorrow something you can do today – especially if that something is saying "I love you".'

'Finally, having you all here today reminds Jeremy and me of just how much love there is in the world. And now that we're married, we intend to make a whole lot more...'

The Father of the Bride's Speech

Traditionally, the father of the bride is the first speaker (apart from a brief introduction from the best man), so your speech is a sort of scene-setter.

The idea behind this is doubtless linked to the fact that the father of the bride was always supposed to foot the bill for the wedding – so if you're paying, you should at least be allowed to get your oar in first!

Note to fathers of the bride

Your daughter has chosen to marry, and it is your duty to send her into married life by celebrating her pre-wedding years in a sentimental – and possibly amusing – way.

You've waited all your life for this moment, so take the time to enjoy it. This is your chance to tell her how much you care for her and let everyone else know how wonderful she is. Make the most of it.

Traditionally, you speak first and:

Thank anyone involved in planning (and paying for) the wedding.
Speak proudly of your daughter and welcome the groom into your family.
Thank everyone for coming.
Propose a toast to the bride and groom.

But you could also:

Make a joint speech with your wife.
Share the stage with a stepfather or godfather.
Simply thank everyone for coming and propose a toast.
Show a short film or candid camera shots of your daughter as a child.

The basics

So what do you have to say?

- Thank the guests for coming to the wedding and being involved in such a special day. Remember to mention anyone who has travelled a long distance.
- Thank anyone who has made some kind of financial contribution to the wedding.
- Tell your daughter how proud you are of her.
- Welcome your new son-in-law into your family.
- Reminisce about your daughter's pre-wedding years.
- Wish the newlyweds success and happiness in the future.
- Propose a toast to the bride and groom.

The father of the bride's speech is generally expected to be the least funny and often the most sentimental, which should make the job of writing it the easiest. But it's not always the case. This speech is often the one that has been anticipated for the longest period of time and is probably if not the most emotional, then certainly the one filled with the most pride. The father of the bride begins the speeches, thus setting the tone for the rest of the proceedings. The best advice is to stay mostly with convention, unless you're feeling particularly brave or imaginative. It's easier to write a speech starting with the traditional component parts: welcoming the guests, thanking everyone, talking about the bride, welcoming the groom and, finally, the toast.

If you know what you'd like to say, but aren't sure how to say it, here are some suggestions with some options to consider incorporating into your speech.

1. The welcome

- Thank you all for coming and sharing this special day with Nicola and John.
- I'd like to take this opportunity to thank you all for being here. I know that some of you have had further to come than others, but you are all welcome guests on this happy day/night.
- Ladies and gentlemen, I'm delighted to see so many of you here today to celebrate the marriage of my daughter Nicola to John.

2. The thanks

- Nicola and John have worked very hard to pay for today, and it's been worth it. This is a lovely meal/reception, and everything looks perfect. I'm proud of the pair of you.

- Weddings are not cheap occasions, but my little girl/ daughter deserves the best and, as you can see, she's got it. This would not have been possible without the generous help of John's parents, George and Amy.

- This wedding has taken a lot of time and patience to organize, and decisions have sometimes been difficult to reach [make a small joke about the struggle it was to decide between a sophisticated colour scheme or an outrageous one of pink with yellow spots], but I'm really delighted that everything's turned out so well. In particular, I'd like to thank the florist/minister/ bridesmaids for the amount of trouble they have gone to. Everything/the church/the hall/the hotel/the bouquet looks/look wonderful.

3. The bride

- I have always known that Nicola is a beautiful woman, but I have never seen her look quite so beautiful or so radiant as she does today. I'm extremely proud of her.
- Nicola has had many roles in life... (for example, daughter, fiancée, student, air hostess, etc.) but never has she looked more beautiful than as a bride.
- When Nicola told me that she was going to get married, I was worried that she wouldn't be my little girl any more, but seeing her today as a beautiful bride, I realize that no matter how old she is she will always be my little girl, and I love her.
- This elegant/beautiful/radiant/lovely bride is a far cry from the Nicola I remember so well, who was always in trouble for being messy/muddy/late/a tomboy/scruffy, but, no matter what she looks like I love her, and am very proud to be her father.

If you're not the bride's father, there are many ways to convey how proud you are to take on this role.

- I am not Nicola's father but I know that he would have been so proud of her today, as I am.
- Nicola has been my comfort and joy, and I am honoured that she chose me to give this speech.
- As Nicola's brother, I am supposed to be nasty to her and pull her hair to remind her that I am older than she is. Trouble is, she looks too gorgeous today. Still, I am very proud to be giving her away on behalf of our family. John, please look after her!

4. Welcome the groom

Here are a few ideas with a number of options to cut and paste into your own speech.

- There are not many men good enough for Nicola, but John is. When she turned up with a scruffy/spotty/runny-nosed/ well-groomed/lanky/large/tall/pony-tailed man, I was suspicious/delighted/dismayed/curious/ welcoming, and/but I never hoped/really hoped that they would marry. And/But they have, and I am really pleased for them. John is a good/delightful/fun/great/ lovely man, and they make a wonderful couple.
- John is one of that rare breed of men – he really is as good/sincere/wonderful/perfect/much of a creep as he appears, and I am absolutely delighted to welcome him into our/my family.
- Nicola always claimed that she would never get married/ find the right man/love anyone/be happy, but she was wrong. In John she has found the perfect partner, and I am delighted he has become a part of my/our family.
- What can I say about John? He is a great/perfect/lovely/ wonderful/good man, and no one else would be as perfect for my daughter/Nicola. I'm delighted that he's decided to become part of the family.

5. General chat

This is your chance to make a few gentle jokes, but nothing crude or offensive. You might even want to quote something or recite a poem.

- Marriage, as I know all too well, is about compromise and to keep things running smoothly it's good to talk. However, as Helen Rowland said, 'Before marriage, a man will lie awake thinking about something you said; after marriage, he'll fall asleep before you finish saying it.'
- The best guarantee for a peaceful marriage is simple – lie. If she asks you if you've done whatever you've forgotten to do, say that you have and then do it. If he catches you doing something you shouldn't, say you did it as a surprise for him. Men are stupid: they'll believe anything, or at least pretend to, for a peaceful life!

- Nicola always said that she'd never find that special someone, but I'm delighted to see that she has. I just want to read something now because it seems so appropriate and expresses exactly what I mean. It's called Destiny and is by Sir Edwin Arnold:

  Somewhere there waiteth in this world of ours
  For one lone soul another lonely soul,
  Each choosing each through all the weary hours
  And meeting strangely at one sudden goal.
  Then blend they, like green leaves with golden flowers,
  Into one beautiful and perfect whole;
  And life's long night is ended, and the way
  Lies open onward to eternal day.

- You may think that this wedding has cost a lot but, as Goethe said, 'The sum which two married people owe to one another defies calculation. It is an infinite debt, which can only be discharged through all eternity.' I wonder if their bank manager would believe that?

- As a certain German philosopher once said: 'To marry is to halve your rights and double your duties', but if that were all there is to it, then none of us would get married in the first place. I'm delighted that Nicola and John have taken the plunge, otherwise none of us would be here enjoying this fine champagne/wine/beer/tap water.

6. The toast

By the time you get to the toast, it's almost time for you to sit down – but not quite. Finish with a flourish and then relax – the rest of the day/evening/night is yours to enjoy!

- Ladies and gentlemen, please be upstanding. I give you… the bride and groom.
- Ladies and gentlemen, please charge your glasses. I give you… the bride and groom.
- Honoured guests, please join me in the traditional toast. I give you… the bride and groom.
- Ladies and gentlemen, please be upstanding and raise your glasses. I give you… the bride and groom.

Any of these sample speeches can be used as a starting point. The most important part to remember, though, is to tell your daughter how much you love her. Be prepared – carry a handkerchief in case you get too emotional!

Sample speeches: A touch of humour

'This is an important day for me. It's certainly not the time for jokes but the time when I resuscitate my bank account and hand over Sarah's spending habits to someone else.

The good thing about weddings is that you can show everyone how generous you are. I wanted to give you all an itemized bill so that you could see for yourselves how much these flowers cost, but Angela told me that it was not the done thing… as she slipped on her £150 hat!

Seriously, I have looked forward to this day for years. Sarah makes a stunning bride and John is a good man, and I wish them every happiness for the future. If they are as happy as my wife and I, then they will be very happy indeed.

Marriage is an important commitment, so much so that you need a mortgage to pay for it! But it takes more than that. It needs patience and compromise, and I should know – I've been patiently compromising for years!

Bob's just looked at his watch, which is the signal that he needs a drink, so, ladies and gentlemen, please be upstanding. I give you… the bride and groom.'

Sample speeches: Short and sweet

'When Sarah was a little girl, she used to lift her dress over her head and pretend it was a veil. Fortunately, she's acquired a bit more finesse since then, and today she is the most beautiful bride I have seen since I married her mother more than 30 years ago. I am so proud that my little girl has grown into such a beautiful and accomplished woman.

This wedding has been a huge family affair and today we become one big family. I'd like to thank John's parents, on behalf of the bride and groom, for their generosity. Without it we would not all be sitting down to such a lovely meal in such a beautiful hotel, and I'm grateful to them for helping to make this day so special for my youngest daughter.

What can I say about John? Quite simply, Sarah couldn't have chosen better. He's everything I would have looked for in a son-in-law and I'm delighted that he's joining our family.

I don't want to bore you with how happy I am today, so I'll finish up with the traditional toast, offered from the heart. Ladies and gentleman, I give you... the bride and groom.'

Weddings can be a very difficult time if a close relative or friend has passed away. Here is an example of one way to honour them in your speech.

Sample speeches: Honouring a deceased relative

'Standing here in front of all of you today, I feel incredibly old. To me, it was only yesterday that Sarah was born, and I never thought that I'd ever be as happy as I was then, but I was wrong. Seeing my daughter look as radiant as she does on her wedding day makes me happier than I ever thought possible. I am so proud of everything that she has become. My only regret is that her mother, Angela, cannot be with us. But this is not a day for regrets – it is a day for happiness and looking ahead.

I am so pleased that Sarah and John found each other. I never thought that anyone would be good enough for my little girl, but I am delighted to be proved wrong. John is a lovely man who makes my daughter happy. What more could I ask?

I don't want to delay the proceedings any longer with my memories of Sarah growing up, like the time when she was almost expelled for trying to burn down her school so she could have a day off – she never was very practical! Instead, I am going to ask you all to be upstanding and join me in a toast. Ladies and gentlemen, please raise your glasses. I give you… the bride and groom.'

Sample speeches: Straight and sentimental

'I'm so pleased you could all be here on this wonderful occasion, which Lisa and David have gone to so much trouble to make absolutely perfect. It's a wonderful start to their married life together, which I know we all hope will be as successful as today is proving to be.

Success in marriage is more than finding the right person – it is being the right person – and I am proud to be here celebrating the marriage of these two lovely people, who are not only amazing in their own right, but are also the right people for each other.

Lisa, over the past ten months when you've been planning this wedding, your mother and I have had plenty of opportunities to observe you demonstrating all those fantastic qualities you have possessed since you were a girl. You have been creative in your planning, patient when things went wrong, generous and helpful to others, intelligent when dealing with difficult situations and a delight to be with. You remind me of your mother.

In short, Lisa has been everything you could want in a daughter, and I can only wish that she and David will be as happy as Mary and I have been during the last 34 years.

Ladies and gentlemen, please charge your glasses and join me in a toast. I give you: the bride and groom!'

Sample speeches: Brief and witty

'Let me just start by saying that I'm delighted to see so many of you here today. There's lots of people I recognize, a few of them looking far more grown up and elegant than usual. I'm talking mainly of course about my children here, and I hope to meet many more of you before the evening ends.

Well I'm going to keep this brief, because [looking at glass] Claire has made me pay for this, and while I'm up here and you're down there, I can't be doing my fair share of drinking! However, Claire has assured me she won't be imbibing too much of the potent stuff today, which I have to say was a relief, to both myself and my bank manager.

This isn't of course the first time my bank manager and I have spoken about keeping Claire in the manner to which she'd like to become accustomed – I seem to remember the pony, tennis camp, was it ballet lessons? Naturally I always said no, because I was determined to bring her up in a disciplined manner, and naturally she always got her own way, rather like today, because she is absolutely irresistible! I'm delighted, too, that Stephen has found her equally irresistible and I am thrilled to welcome him to the family.

I know other people want to say a few words, so Claire, Stephen, can I just say that you are two wonderful people and I hope you have a wonderful life together. Ladies and gentlemen, please join me in a toast to the bride and groom!'

Sample speeches: She wears the trousers

'It will come as no surprise to you, Adam, that Sara was nicknamed "Miss Bossy Boots" at school. Looking back, I suppose she was displaying her leadership abilities even then. She certainly led my wife and me up the garden path many a time!

Sara was always strong-willed. Even as a child, if there was something she wanted, she didn't stop until she got it. So, Adam, I guess you didn't stand a chance. But then again, where would Adam be without someone there to run his life for him?

Tomboy she used to be, lady she is now. But don't be fooled by that beautiful smile. Sara is a formidable opponent. Woe betide anyone who disagrees with her. Ladies and gentlemen, I'm afraid you'll have to forgive me for the following gap in my speech – Sara edited the next bit out and I'm under strict instructions not to mention… er, sorry, that's been crossed out too.'

Toasts given by the father of the bride

The father of the bride traditionally toasts the bride and groom at the end of his speech.

Traditional

'I end my speech today by thanking you all for joining us to celebrate the wedding of Annabel and Ben. It's been a wonderful day so far and we hope this will be the beginning of a wonderful life together for them. Please join me in wishing them all the best… To Annabel and Ben!'

Bit of banter

'Before we raise our glasses, John, I'd like you to take Diana's hand and place your own over it. Now remember and cherish this special moment, because believe me, if I know my daughter, this is the last time you'll have the upper hand… To Diana and John!'

Quick quip

'Apparently, my wife tells me, I'm now supposed to make toast. Good grief! Haven't you all eaten enough already? Ah, right, I see, I'm supposed to make a toast. Well, then, please stand and raise your glasses quickly before I mess anything else up and join with me in wishing John and Emma every happiness… To the bride and groom!'

A traditional approach

'Today is all about two people and their decision to spend the rest of their lives together. We wish them good luck and great joy, today and always. So please stand and raise your glasses with me... To the happy couple!'

Getting sentimental

'It's said that when children find true love, parents find true joy – and true joy is what I am feeling today. As a father, whatever else I may have wanted for my children, my abiding wish has always been for them to find relationships in which they can be truly happy. I know Katie has found this with Daniel. Katie, as everyone knows, is the apple of my eye.

So for me to say that I have gained a wonderful son-in-law is the greatest compliment that I can give. Ladies and gentlemen, I would like you to join me in drinking a toast to the happy couple. Please be upstanding and raise your glasses to Katie and Daniel.'

For more sample toasts, see page 162.

The Groom's Speech

You will say the most important words of the day, if not your life, when you say 'I do'.

Now it's your chance to thank everybody and tell your bride how much you love her, and in front of everybody you know.

Daunted? Don't be – everybody is there because they want to be. They've chosen to spend their free time watching you marry the woman you love and, for once, the focus is not on her dress but on you.

Note to grooms

Traditionally, you speak second and:

Thank the father of the bride for his (hopefully) kind comments!

Thank the wedding organizers/mums – often with bouquets.

Thank everyone for being there.

Compliment your new wife.

Toast the bridesmaids, often giving them a gift.

But you don't have to stick with tradition. You could:

Let the bride speak instead, or do the speech together.

Read out a poem that sums up how you feel about the day.

Simply toast those who helped with the wedding, but don't make a speech.

Remember that if your bride is not going to give a speech, all your words should be from both of you. Bear this in mind throughout your speech – you don't want to just include your new wife in a single section of it as if you'd only just remembered to bung her in at the last minute! Oh – and beginning your speech 'My wife and I…' usually provokes an immediate audience reaction!

Where to start

So, what is expected of the groom?

- The first task is to thank your new father-in-law for his speech and for his beautiful daughter.
- Thank the guests for sharing your day and for their generous gifts.
- Thank both sets of parents for their help with the wedding celebrations.
- Give a small gift to the two mothers. (For some suggestions, see www.confetti.co.uk)
- Compliment your new wife!
- Thank the best man for his help, and give your gifts to him and to the rest of the bridal party.
- Raise a glass and offer a toast to the bridesmaids.

Here are some useful phrases and ideas for a great groom's speech. All you need to do is pick the best ones for you and fill in the blanks!

1. Thank your new father-in-law

- I just want to thank my father-in-law for his kind/generous/special words. I feel honoured that he has taken/welcomed me into his family.
- Thank you, Ken, for your kind/generous/sweet/special words. It is good to know how you feel about Sarah and me getting married.
- My wife and I would like to thank Ken for being the best father of the bride ever. Not only did he give her away instead of locking her in her room, but his kind/sweet/generous/witty words have also made me feel welcome as the newest member of his family.
- My wife and I want to thank Ken for his witty/kind/generous/sincere words. I now feel embarrassed about everything I said about him in the past/justified in my opinion that he's a great/good/perfect father-in-law. What can I say after that speech? Thanks, Ken.

2. Thank your guests

- This is the most important day of our lives, and my wife and I/Sarah and I/we are delighted to share it with so many friends and family/our closest friends and families/two complete strangers in a register office. We are also very grateful that so many of you have not only gone to the expense of sharing this day with us but have also bought us presents. Thank you.

- I can't believe that you all made it here. You really are the best bunch/group/lot/mob/pack/herd of friends and family that we could ever hope to have. So thank you. We're also extremely grateful for the presents. Sarah was saying only a couple of days ago that she really wanted another toaster... or two!

3. Thank your in-laws

- I am so delighted/pleased/honoured/relieved/happy
to have Ken and Angela as my new family/in-laws/other Mum
and Dad. I knew that I'd like/love/get on with/adore them
when I fell in love with Sarah because they have helped her
to be the person she is – perfect/rich/ wonderful/fond of
beer and rugby!

4. Compliment your wife!

- You are always beautiful but you have never looked as
stunning/good/wonderful/gorgeous as you do today.
You make the most wonderful/stunning/gorgeous/perfect
bride. I love you.
- I was expecting to feel nervous/sick/terrified/concerned/
worried/frightened when I woke up today but I didn't. Why?
Because I knew that you would be walking down that aisle
towards me and that the only thing I wanted was for you to
be my wife/us to be married. I knew that you would look
lovely – you always do – but today you are radiant/gorgeous/
beautiful/wonderful/fantastic/stunning/a vision/perfect/the
perfect bride. You mean so much to me, and I want to thank
you for agreeing to become my wife. I am so proud/happy/
honoured to be your husband, and I love you very much.

- Sarah, you are a beautiful/stunning/radiant/gorgeous/ lovely bride, and I know that you are just as beautiful on the inside. When we first met, I realized that you were the most beautiful woman in the world/were the only woman for me/had a ladder in your stockings, but I never thought/imagined/dared to hope that you would marry me. I am so happy/chuffed/delighted/ecstatic/ proud that you agreed to be my wife and share the rest of your life with me. I've been so proud of the way you have juggled organizing this wedding with your job/ everything else and have still been patient and understanding. Now, I just want to say, in front of our friends and family, how much you mean to me. I love you.

The first time I saw Hannah I was dazzled by her. If you had told me then that we would one day be married, I wouldn't have believed you – although I would have wanted to. I can honestly say that I don't think anyone could be as happy as I am today. I'm immensely proud to be able to call her my wife. What I really love about our relationship is that we make a really great team. We trust and support one another, and we each know that, come what may, the other will be there for them. I know that marriage is not all fun and laughter like today, but I know too that my wife and I have the strength to deal with any difficulties that life may throw at us.

5. Thank your bride

- I never thought I could be as happy as I am today without England/Wales/Scotland/Ireland winning the Six Nations. Roz, you've made me feel like I've scored the winning try/kicked a critical drop goal in the match of my life. You're my Twickenham/Millennium Stadium/Murrayfield/Lansdowne Road, and right now I feel like cheering because I'm just over the moon you've married me. I know there will be times when you send me for an early bath/to sit in the sin bin. But I also know that, just like supporting Bath, it's something that stays with you for life, through the ups and downs, and you just can't change that. Roz, I'm your biggest fan, and I love you.

(You can amend the above to reflect your favourite sport – but only use it if it's not a sore spot with the bride!)

6. Thank the best man

- When I asked Sarah to marry me, I knew that I needed a best man and that there was only one man that title could be given to. Bob is my brother and also a friend/ has been my best friend since school/1972/we met in the sandpit/he stole my BMX, and I knew that he would be perfect for the job. I would like to thank him for all the work he's done today – acting as toastmaster/not losing the rings/getting me to the church on time/ finding my trousers – and for his efforts before the wedding when he listened to me as I raved about the latest waistcoat/buttonhole/wedding dress I had seen. Bob, you've been great/a mate/the best man I could have chosen/cool/a pal/a true friend/gorgeous!
- I get the fun parts of today, but Bob has all the stressful parts. As he's the local postie/hippo-keeper/accountant/ general layabout, I knew that he would be more than able to cope with today and keep everything, especially me, ticking along smoothly.

7. Thank and toast the bridesmaids

- The giggling little posse/stunning group of beautiful bridesmaids over there/to my right/to my left/in front of you have been amazing. Not only did they manage to walk down the aisle without falling over, but they've also been great with all the preparations. It may seem unfair to the rest of you, as you've all been so great/helpful/amazing/bored rigid, but I'd particularly like to thank Vikki for all her hard work. I understand that Sarah's dress would not be looking quite so beautiful/stunning/together/white as it does now were it not for a timely intervention! Ladies and gentleman, I'd like you all to charge/raise your glasses. I give you… the bridesmaids.

- My wife and I/Sarah and I would like to say a special thank you to the bridesmaids, who have been a tower of strength throughout the preparations/day. They've been great/wonderful/beautiful, and little Anna has been so good/patient/sweet and looks gorgeous/adorable/very grown up in her dress. Ladies and gentlemen, please charge/raise your glasses. I give you… the bridesmaids.

Sample speeches: Sweet and loving

'As Jane Austen, or was it Bridget Jones, said 'It is a truth universally acknowledged that a single man in possession of a good fortune must be in want of a good wife.'

Now much as I like to think I am Mr Darcy, and that only bouncing a few cheques to the florist for today establishes me as a man of good fortune, my real good fortune in life is undoubtedly meeting and marrying my wife, Chloe.

She certainly, as somebody else said, has a price beyond rubies, and I'd like to thank my new father-in-law for his kind words and his making me the richest man in the world by letting me marry her.

You have all helped make today the happiest day of our lives by being here with us and being kind enough to bring gifts. I never knew that toasters came in so many varieties! Seriously, the greatest gift to us is your being here, and I hope that you enjoy the day half as much as we are.

My wife (I love saying that!) would not be the person she is without the love and support of her parents, and I want to thank them for helping her to be her and for welcoming me into their family. As my new mother-in-law said, she is not losing a daughter but gaining a washer-upper. While not quite so useful, I hope that she will accept this small gift as a sign of how much I appreciate her love and support.'

Sample speeches: she wears the trousers

'My wife wears the trousers. Beautifully. And as you can see, she looks great in a dress too.'

I should have realized the first time I met Anita what I was letting myself in for. Not only did she insist that she bought the drinks, she drove me home, told me I was to phone her, told me when to phone her, then gave me a full account of what she expected me to say when I did phone her. Well, I've always enjoyed a bit of domination!

Some people call my wife "bossy". I call her "ma'am". No, seriously – I call her strong and independent, and am honoured to have her as my companion.

Anita, I just want to say, in front of our families and dearest friends, that I love you and hope that every day will be as happy as today – just not as expensive.

Not only did Bob, my old roommate from Uni days and the best man I know, get me to the church on time but he also didn't lose the ring. I'm grateful for everything that he's done for me and look forward to returning the compliment – as soon as possible.

Lastly, I would like to thank the pack of bridesmaids, who have been such good friends throughout all the preparations. Ladies and gentlemen, please be upstanding. I give you… the bridesmaids.'

Sample speeches: Short and sweet

'Having listened to such words of wisdom from my new father-in-law, I can only hope that I am worthy of them. Thank you, Ken.

I'm really pleased that you could all make it here today, but I'm especially grateful to the Johnsons, who've travelled all the way from Edinburgh to be with us. I knew that it was worth including the words "free bar" on the invitations!

You've all been very generous, not only by being here today to share this happy occasion, but also by giving us so many wonderful gifts.

My parents brought me up to believe that good things come to those who wait, and I want to thank them for being right and for being there whenever I needed them, especially this morning when Dad helped me do up my tie as I was shaking so much. Thanks, both of you.

I now have a new set of parents, the in-laws. Contrary to all the horror stories, mine are amazing, but I always knew that they would be as no one could raise so perfect a woman as my wife if they weren't wonderful themselves. I want to thank them for helping us to have the best wedding we could ever have dreamed of. Thank you, Ken and Angela, for your kindness and for raising such a beautiful daughter.'

'Sarah, no one could have made me as happy as you have these last few years, and I look forward to growing old and grey with you.

And going grey is something that almost happened prematurely when we were on the way to the church and Bob realized that he'd left the ring behind. Fortunately everything else went according to plan, and it was great to have my best man at my side.

As for the bridesmaids, what can I say except they look lovely and have been great through all the preparations? I'd like them to accept these small offerings with our love. They deserve a drink so, ladies and gentlemen, please be upstanding. I give you… the bridesmaids.'

Sample speeches: Second marriages

'This is a second marriage for both of us, and I am grateful for the words my new father-in-law has just spoken. Sarah and I feel privileged to have found each other and to be given a second chance of love.

My parents have been particularly supportive over the last few weeks when wedding nerves set in, but this was to be expected as they've always been there for me, no matter what. I know that Sarah feels the same about her parents, who have welcomed me into their family and have been so generous, helping us with this wedding.

When I first met Sarah I thought that she was a beautiful woman but I never thought I'd see her again. Fortunately, thanks to some matchmaking by Bob, my best man and the father of Billy, our excellent pageboy who only tried to eat the cushion once, we did see each other again. I'd like to thank him for helping us get where we are today. Sarah and I will always be grateful for his interference!

Sarah believes strongly that looks are less important than personality, which is just as well, otherwise she wouldn't have agreed to marry me! Sarah has taught me the importance of patience and compromise as our families have united to make a whole, and I am grateful to her that she has helped me make this transition quite so easily. Standing here today, in front of you all, I have to say that it has definitely been worth it.'

Sample speeches: Second marriages

Obviously our wedding would be nothing without the love and blessing of our children, Claire, David and Simon. Claire has told me confidentially, so you'll have to keep this to yourselves, that she's always wanted a brother. So now that she's got two, I hope that she'll be twice as happy. David and Simon, I'd like to say how delighted I am to be your step-father. And Claire, Sarah has asked me to say that you are the daughter she thought she would never have.

Kate's daughter, Vikki, has been a tower of strength through all the pre-wedding stress. So for that and for your fantastic flower arrangements, thank you, Vikki. So, please raise your glasses to… Vikki.

Sample speeches: How to include children of a previous marriage

- I've always been terribly grateful to Sara's children, Fiona and Jack. Sarah's experience raising them has surely made her more prepared to take me on, although I do promise to clean my room and do my homework from now on.
- I'm delighted that my son John and Sasha's daughter Melanie are here to share today – and the rest of our lives – with us.
- I count myself doubly lucky that the young lady over there, Tina, Geraldine's daughter, can be with us today. It is a delight and a privilege to know her, and thank you, Tina, for all the help you've given us preparing for this wedding.

Toasts given by the groom

The groom traditionally toasts the bridesmaids/maid of honour. He may also choose to toast his wife, and his wife will then reply and toast the bridesmaids. He may also toast the hosts, traditionally his new in-laws, especially if there are no bridesmaids.

Edible joke

'Apparently I'm now supposed to toast our hosts, my parents-in-law. That's a bit of a shame because I think I'd rather have them spit-roasted with onions and lots of garlic. Oh, that kind of toast. Awfully sorry, Mr and Mrs Johnson: you know I think you're good enough to eat! To Mr and Mrs Johnson, ladies and gentlemen!'

Thanks, ladies

'I'd like to take this opportunity to thank the bridesmaids for their sterling work. I've discovered that for an occasion like this, you really do need to have experts on table flowers, leg-waxing, eyelash-curling and themed party favours on hand, and Alice, Hannah and Ellen certainly fit the bill. They really have been essential in making this a perfect day. Ladies and gentlemen, please raise your glasses to the bridesmaids.'

One for the parents

'A wedding is a coming together of two families, and I couldn't
have wished to join a friendlier family than Stella's, so I'd like
to end my speech by thanking our hosts and my new parents-
in-law, Betty and Stan, for making this such a wonderful
occasion. It's often said that wedding days belong to the happy
couple, but there are many people who have helped to make
today so perfect. I'd also like to thank my parents, Pauline and
Max, for everything they've done for us. Without the hard
work of our parents, Stella and I wouldn't have been able to
concentrate on having such a good time today! Please raise
your glasses to them.'

Love lines

'I'd like to end my speech by proposing a toast to my bride.
Without wishing to embarrass anyone by getting too
sentimental, Charlotte is all I have ever dreamed of. Someone
once said that to love is to receive a glimpse of heaven. Well, I
feel I am truly in heaven today… Please raise your glasses to
the beautiful bride.'

For more sample toasts, see page 162.

The Best Man's Speech

The best man's speech is often the most eagerly anticipated and attentively listened to of all.

So it's not surprising that making the speech has become the centrepiece of the best man's role and is likely to dominate the way in which you prepare for the big day.

Notes for the Best Man

Your role, in short, is a multiple one. As the groom's best friend, you will be expected to subject him to an ordeal of gentle embarrassment. As host, you will read out telegrams and pass on any practical announcements. And as traditional head of the wedding assistants, you will also speak on behalf of the bridesmaids.

In accordance with tradition...
Of course you'll want to make your speech as entertaining as possible, but traditionally the best man's speech is also expected to cover certain points and fulfil certain functions.

Traditionally, for instance, the best man will...
- Introduce all the other speakers, unless there is a toastmaster. Nowadays, speakers can be quite numerous as more people often choose to speak.
- Read any messages from friends and family who haven't been able to attend.
- Propose a toast to the bride and groom.

Your speech will also be expected to include...
- Thanks to the groom for his toast to the bridesmaids.
- Comments on the happy couple, particularly the groom.
- Comments on how great the day has been.
- Thanks to the organizers.

Last but not least

Speeches are traditionally given in a certain order:

- Father of the bride
- Groom
- Best man

It's becoming more usual for other people to make a speech, too – the mother of the bride and chief bridesmaid, for example, might also want to say a few words. But however many people speak, the best man traditionally always goes last – saving the best till then, hopefully.

Good timing

Speeches are usually made after the main meal, so by the time the best man comes to make his, the guests tend to have relaxed considerably (a fact not unconnected with the wine that will be disappearing from the tables). This can often work in your favour, as by now the guests will be nicely warmed up and well disposed to laugh at your jokes.

However, this can also mean that you end up spending the meal feeling nervous – or worse, over-indulging in the name of Dutch courage. A drink or two may help steady your nerves, but don't overdo it: a slurred speech will be remembered for all the wrong reasons!

Here are some useful phrases and ideas for a best man's speech. All you need to do is pick the best ones for you and fill in the blanks!

1. The thanks

You represent the other members of the bridal party (i.e. the bridesmaids and ushers), so the first thing you have to say is easy – thank the groom for his words about the bridesmaids.

- Ladies and gentlemen, I would like to thank the groom for his kind/generous/short/patronizing/lying words about the lovely/giggling/drunken/fabulous bridesmaids.

2. Who are you?

Let everyone know how you and the groom first met each other and how you feel about being his best man.

- When I first met John on our first day at school/Uni/ prison/work, I thought that he was a good bloke/a con man/an idiot/an alcoholic/a lucky man to meet me, but I never realized that I would end up, all these years later, being his best man. I have to say that I was honoured/ staggered/horrified/shocked/drunk when he asked me, but I'm delighted/honoured/pleased/drunk again/terrified to be here today in front of all of you.

3. About the groom

- John has always been a good bloke/an idiot/a generous man, even when [say when you met, e.g., first day of school] and he [recount a funny incident or use one of his pet phrases; don't cause offence but be funny]. I can't believe that he's finally/actually married.
- When John asked me to be his best man I thought that he had no other friends/his Mum had made him ask me, and I was honoured/terrified. Now that I'm here, I'm even more so.
- The man who wouldn't commit/buy pizza for more than one/share his remote control/even consider a joint bank account is now married!
- I never thought that I'd live to see this day. I've known John since [say how you met and when] and I'm delighted/stunned/pleased/shocked/really happy for him and even more shocked at/horrified at/staggered by/terrified by/committed to being his best man – as he is the best man I've ever known.

4. Tell an amusing/sweet anecdote about the groom

You're his best man for a reason, so delve into your mutual past and tell an amusing anecdote. Hopefully, the only difficulty doing this will be trying to decide which tale to tell. If it's not that easy, the following might trigger a few memories – just remember to keep it short and clean!

- Thinking up an original excuse for being late/not handing in his homework/project.
- First time you had a boy's night out and he decided that he wanted to be a morris dancer.
- Any dreams of unsuitable jobs, e.g. pilot, stripper [unless he was!], train/racing driver [and recently had a minor scrape in his car], pop star [and can't sing], etc.
- Cooking anecdotes always work. The late Dame Barbara Cartland once said that 90% of marriages end because of bad cooking: even if he didn't blow up a microwave by putting a whole egg in it, he must have had some kind of cooking disaster – we all have. As the 19th-century novelist George Meredith said, 'Kissing don't last: cookery do!'

5. Don't forget the bride

Always make a point of saying something nice about the bride.
This is the woman who will let your friend/brother
still go out to play with the lads, so start off on the right foot.
You know you want to!

- Sarah/Mrs Finn is the luckiest woman/girl for marrying John today but, looking at her, I can understand why he chose her. She's a beautiful/stunning/gorgeous/lovely/radiant bride.
- Sarah, what can I say? You look beautiful/lovely/stunning/ radiant and you deserve each other/make a beautiful couple/are perfect for each other.
- When John first introduced me to Sarah, my first reaction was that she was too good/perfect/ideal for him. I'm delighted to see them here together today and wish them every happiness for the future.

6. Telegram time

A simple rule: explain who all the telegrams are from. Bill and Joy Patterson may mean nothing to many people, and saying Uncle Bill and Aunt Joy from Scotland will make it easier for everyone.

7. Almost there – the final toast

It's nearly time to sit down, but not just yet. This is the easy bit and your audience will be delighted to participate. Decide with the bride and groom beforehand if people should stand up or not. If they should, ask them to 'be upstanding'.

- Ladies and gentlemen, please be upstanding and raise/ charge your glasses. I give you… the bride and groom.
- Ladies and gentlemen, please join me in a toast. I give you… the bride and groom.

Dos and don'ts

- Never swear or use offensive words, even if they do crop up in everyday speech.
- Always think of an old granny sitting in the corner when you write your speech, and try not to give her a heart attack or make her blush!
- Don't try too hard to be funny.
- Avoid saying anything you wouldn't want anyone to know if it were about you, and you can't go wrong.
- Make a note of anyone you want to thank or mention. You might find it easiest to write down your speech, for either glancing at or as reassurance, or use little revision cards with bullet point reminders.
- Decide if you want to read some cards or telegrams during your speech. If you do, be sure to arrange for a family member to collect them together for you.
- Practise, practise, practise!
- Never make fun of the wedding, even if you dislike the venue, colour scheme, even the bride's dress.
- Avoid potentially difficult and embarrassing subjects such as having children (in case it turns out that they can't), drug problems (in case either the bride or the families don't know about it), excessive partying or womanizing while seeing the bride (ditto), money problems (ditto) or previous girlfriends (need we say more?).

Sample speeches: The not-so-squeaky-clean groom

'Ben has always been an entrepreneur. But at school the teachers didn't really respect his commercial spirit. While he considered his money-making enterprises demonstrated creative thinking and immense initiative, his suspension certificate chose to describe it as "extortion".'

'Ben is a man with a past. He's been there, done that, worn the T-shirt. His philosophy has always been: try everything once, and if you enjoy it, try it again. He's flirted with the law (and a few WPCs when necessary); he's broken a few hearts and he's caused a few blushes. But at the end of the day, he'd lay his life on the line for the people he loves. He's been a true friend to me for 20 years, and I know he'll be the most loyal, devoted husband to Mandy for the rest of their lives.'

'My friendship with Ben dates back to our first day at secondary school. I was immediately drawn to him because he looked like the cool one. I'm not sure if it was his bleached blonde hair or his skin-tight trousers that made him stand out from the crowd, or his huge badge collection and his Masters of the Universe backpack. Man, that boy had style! Best of all, his attitude earned the reputation of school rebel. He refused to wear black socks. He did his homework in biro. And once he even cracked a test tube on purpose. He was wild!'

Sample speeches: Not always a bed of roses

'As we all know, Chris is a highly successful businessman now. But that hasn't always been the case. In fact his early forays into employment were a disaster. He was fired from his paper round when his boss found out he'd used the papers to make a life-size papier mâché dinosaur for a school project. He got a verbal warning from the landlord of the Dog and Duck for downing a yard of ale every time a customer said to him "have one for yourself". And his milk round came to an abrupt halt when he was arrested for float rage.'

'Life hasn't always been a bed of roses for Chris and Kate. Although you might think butter wouldn't melt in his mouth, he's had to do a fair bit of grovelling to get to where he is today. On their first date Chris got so drunk that, at the end of the night, he gave £20 to Kate and his phone number to the cab driver.'

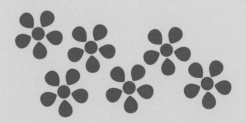

Sample speeches: 'The appraisal'

'Ladies and gentlemen, it really is an honour to be standing in front of you today as best man to someone as special as Gary [the groom]. I must say that when he asked me, I was totally taken aback. But now I'm standing here I feel nothing but pride. Thanks for such an honour, mate.

'Okay, that was the nice, sincere part of the speech. Now it's time to get down to the nitty-gritty of embarrassing the very man who showed such faith, and yet such poor judgment, in choosing me.

'I thought long and hard about how to theme this speech, and then it suddenly dawned on me that I could use the skills I've picked up as a manager at work. I thought I'd write Katy [the bride] an appraisal of Gary.

'So, first things first: punctuality. Well, Katy, you must have known Gary long enough by now to know that he is not the world's greatest timekeeper. In fact, he's not the world's best when it comes to dates either. Only last week he told me how much he was looking forward to the wedding – on 7 July! Luckily I corrected him and here we are on the 8th… just! We were running late for most of the stag do, too, when Gary managed to miss the train to his own party. So Katy, you have been warned.

'Next we move on to: management skills. As we all know, one of the prerequisites of being a good manager is the art of diplomacy. And I think it's fair to say that Gary is not a man overly blessed with skills in this particular area. I remember we were sitting in French class when we were about 15 and we had a new teacher, Miss Simpson. She had just introduced herself and we were asking her some questions before class began when Gary piped up and asked her when her baby was due. Of course, there was no baby. Poor old, plump Miss Simpson went bright red and the rest of the class fell about. You did rather poorly in your 'O' level French, as I recall, Gary…

'Next on the agenda, Katy, has to be: career prospects. Now Gary is, as I'm sure we'll all agree, very competent at his job. In fact, he has moved steadily through the ranks and is doing very nicely, thanks. But I must say that things could have been so different. I'm told that during his student days, his part time career at a large drinks company [alter as appropriate] was marred by his performance at the first Christmas party he attended all those years ago. Let's look at the ingredients of the disaster, shall we? There was Mr Hobbs [the groom], women and there was a free bar. Needless to say, Mr Hobbs helped himself to the bar, got rather drunk and rather loud and managed to finish the evening off by falling asleep on a desk, with his trousers neatly folded on the back of the chair. Sadly, it wasn't his desk – or chair – but his boss's. Oh, dear…

'Now what about: teamwork? Gary has always been a great team player. He's run the line for pretty much every football team he's tried to play in. He's washed the kit for several rugby clubs he's tried to join, and he makes a cracking tea when the lads play Sunday afternoon cricket. But seriously, though, Gary thrives in a team environment. He's unselfish and supportive when things are going badly, and that's what makes him such a great bloke. He can't play sport for toffee, mind you, but he's a great mascot…

'And finally, Katy, we move on to: extra-curricular activities. There's no point in denying that Gary thought of himself as a bit of a ladies' man at college. It turned out, however, that he was only chatting up different girls all the time because he couldn't find one that was interested. His favourite chat-up line at the time was: "We don't need to take our clothes off to have a good time. Let's just drink some cherry wine."
I rest my case.

'So, Katy, that's my appraisal of Gary. It's too late to back out now. You'll just have to make a fist of it and see what happens. But what I do know is that he loves you very much and that you're going to have a great life together. To the happy couple!'

Sample speeches: About the groom

'Nick and I have been friends since primary school. I think we bonded on our first day because we were the only two kids in the playground who spoke Klingon. I even thought he'd come in character, but I now see those ears are hereditary. Sorry, Mr Johnston.'

'When Nick was a kid, he wasn't much to look at. Crazy as it may sound today, when he was a boy he could break mirrors just by looking in them. I don't know who cut his hair back then, but whoever it was obviously had a grudge. But miracles do happen and, as you can see, time (not to mention a great deal of expensive cosmetic surgery) has turned our ugly duckling into a swan.'

'Nick and I were always getting into trouble when we were young. Actually, let me rephrase that. I was always getting in to trouble while Nick would get away with blue murder. He's always been able to charm his way out of a mess and often ended up with an apology from his victims. So what was the little artful dodger's secret? Perhaps his father – an estate agent – could explain.'

'As many of you know, David and I were at university together. We even read the same subject. Sadly, that's where the similarity ends. He's going places. I'm not. So Lucinda, count yourself lucky you ended up being chatted up by him and not me at that fateful first meeting. Otherwise you could have been heading for Clacton, not the Caribbean, for your honeymoon.'

'Since he first met Lucinda, David has really started to go places. It was "to hell" when he first asked her out, "on your bike" when he tried to coax her into the bedroom, "to the hairdresser's" when he first met her parents – and, of course, when he proposed… to the most expensive jeweller's in town.'

'There's only been one occasion in the history of my friendship with David when his self-confidence has taken a dive. During a game of conkers, a particularly energetic swing from me accidentally took his two front teeth out. Poor old David was beside himself, thinking that people would forever more be shouting "Mind the gap!" and laughing in his face. Ultimately, I managed to convince him that he could still lead a normal life despite his impediment, and he picked himself up, dusted himself down and soon reverted back into the precocious little so-and-so we all know and love. Little did I realize then just how well David would bounce back, managing to get his teeth into someone as ravishing as Lucinda.'

Classic best man's toasts

'So I'd like you all to charge your glasses and join me in toasting the new Mr and Mrs Brown. Ladies and gentlemen, I give you the bride and groom.'

'Wishing them all the health, wealth and happiness in the world, I'd like you all to join me in toasting the happy couple. Ladies and gentlemen, the bride and groom.'

'Now it only remains for me to get you all on your feet. And with charged glasses [pause], I'd like you to join me in toasting the new Mr and Mrs Roberts. Ladies and gentlemen, I give you the wonderful bride and groom.'

'And now all I have left to do is to say what a privilege it is to ask you all to charge your glasses and – for those of you who still can! – rise to your feet. Ladies and gentlemen – the bride and groom.'

'Ladies and gentlemen, will you please join me now in toasting two young – well, quite young! – people who have everything, because [looks at couple] you love each other. Ladies and gentlemen, the lucky couple.'

'To finish with some words from the bard: "Love comforteth like sunshine after rain." So, you two, I hope your marriage is full of intermittent drizzle, followed by days of blistering heat. To the bride and groom.'

'To the adorable couple – Mark and Lisa.'

'Jerry – my best friend – some words of advice in the form of a wise old poem. "To keep a marriage brimming with love in the loving cup, when you are wrong, admit it, and when you are right, shut up!" To Jerry and Claire!'

'Here's to the two things that – without doubt – make a great marriage. Here's to a good sense of humour, and selective hearing. Ladies and gentlemen – the bride and groom.'

'Before we toast the happy couple, here's to wives and lovers everywhere – and to them never, ever meeting!'

For more sample toasts, see page 162.

The Bride's Speech

As the bride, you have the most interesting role of all when it comes to the speeches. The other main speeches – the father of the bride, best man and so on – have huge traditions attached to them. But, if you decide to make a speech, there will be no such expectations upon you.

More and more brides now choose to give a personal speech, and it can be a great way of mopping up any forgotten thank yous.

When's your turn?

Traditionally, neither the bride nor the chief bridesmaid speaks at a wedding, but more and more are choosing to do so. In this case it is usual for the bride to speak just before or after the groom, while the chief bridesmaid either follows or precedes the best man.

If your father is not present, then you may want to speak first of all, in the traditional father-of-the-bride slot. Some couples opt to stand up and speak together (in many ways a very logical choice); others prefer to speak separately, with each addressing different themes (the other's family, for instance). Or you may prefer to speak after your husband, or even after the best man, as the very last speaker.

Where to start

So, what is expected of the bride?

- Thank everyone who's attending, especially long-lost friends and people who've travelled a long way.
- Thank those people who've supported you through the stress of preparing for the wedding.
- A special word about your mum, not just to thank her for her role in the wedding preparations, but to describe your relationship with her over the years.
- If you like, you could echo the pattern of your new husband's speech: how you met; your first impressions; things you liked and didn't like about him; how the relationship developed; your thoughts on love and marriage; a more personal message from you to him.
- Thank your guests for all their gifts (if the groom hasn't done so already).
- If you are thanking other people, it might make more sense for you, rather than the groom, to thank the bridesmaids.
- A popular American innovation is for the bride to finish with a toast to the guests.

Sample speeches: About the groom

'I grew up in the same street as Robbie so I've known him since we were about eight. In fact, my friends and I used to keep scores on who we thought were the most fanciable boys in the street. Even then Robbie got the highest marks. Maybe it was his Marc Bolan perm, or his wispy moustache, or the way he could burn rubber on his moped. Or maybe it was because he was the only boy over ten in our street.'

'When we were kids, Robbie refused to speak to me – or any other girls for that matter. He only liked cowboys and Indians, and builders, and motorbikes and the police and the army. Well, it was good enough for the Village People, so who am I to judge?'

'Robbie's sister has been kind enough to share some of his childhood photos with me. His first potty training accident… his school sports day… his FIRST GIRLFRIEND! Now you know I'm not the jealous type but… She's blonde, she's cute, she's got a great smile, she's obviously mad about him and you can tell from the way she wore her nappy that the kid had style.'

'When I was first introduced to Barry, I was told that he loved cooking. As someone who has to refer to Delia to boil an egg, I knew I had to have him. I imagined breakfasts in bed, candlelit dinners and romantic picnics, all created by the love of my life. What more could a girl want? Unfortunately, what his mates failed to tell me is that it's not so much cooking he's mad about, as stuffing his face and swooning over Nigella Lawson!'

'I'll admit I had some ulterior motives when I first met Barry. It wasn't his gorgeous blue eyes that attracted me. Nor his rugged handsomeness. I'll confess it was his Workmate (his Black & Decker Workmate, not his colleague, I hasten to add!). The thing is, I needed some shelves doing and he looked keen, willing and able. OK, so the house is now immaculate, but his hands are like sandpaper, he's always putting his back out and he's developed an allergy to paint stripper. Roll on the honeymoon!'

Sample speeches: Short and fun

'I feel like a winner on Oscar night – there are so many people to thank. I just want to reiterate all the thanks that have gone on before. Mum and Dad, you've been great, as have my new in-laws. Thanks to Bob and Vikki, who've helped us to hold this wedding together, and to all of you for just being here, especially that noisy group in the corner who grew up with me and remember how often I said I'd never get married. But, most of all, I'd like to thank John for asking me to marry him and then going through with it!

You've all been so kind saying how nice I look, but I just wanted to say how gorgeous John looks today in his suit. You're great, darling.

I know you all want to get back to the champagne, so I'll leave you to it, but thanks so much for being here and making our day so special.

I'd like you all to raise your glasses and drink a toast… to friends and family.'

Sample speeches: Thanks

'No surprise I'm making a speech, since, as most of you will know, I like to have my say! Which is partly why my mother deserves extra special thanks for helping us organize today in spite of all the arguments. As usual she managed to calm me down and make today perfect. Thank you so much, mum.'

'I'd like to thank a whole host of people, including of course both Daniel and my parents – without whom we'd be sitting in the park eating fish and chips off our laps today! Also to my darling sister, whose legendary calming influence has been invaluable on so many occasions during the wedding-planning process! A special thank you also to Uncle Ron, whose generosity with his beautiful car meant that not only did I get to the church in style and on time, but also that I avoided the amused looks of strangers on the number 13 bus!'

'There is an unsung heroine of this wedding. I'd really like to say a few words of thanks to Carmen who made the beautiful dress I'm wearing. Carmen, without your skill and vision, I can't imagine that today would have been half as enjoyable. Throughout the whole dress-making saga you kept reassuring me that it would all be all right, and though I didn't believe you then, watching Ross's face light up as I walked down the aisle, I was so glad I listened to you. Thanks.'

Sample speeches: Coming together

'Wow – what a lot of people! But at least I know you're a friendly audience. I'd like to thank you all so much for coming here today to take part in the celebration of our marriage. Weddings are real family occasions, and it's lovely to see so many aunts, uncles and cousins here, many of whom I haven't seen for an awfully long time – although I do wish some of you would stop patting me on the head and remarking on how much I've grown.'

'I'd like to thank everyone who's complimented me on my dress and I have to say that, in the words of the song, you're all looking wonderful tonight. I never realized I had such well-dressed, good-looking family and friends. There's definitely some Kate Mosses and Brad Pitts out there.'

'Today, all the important people in my life are here. My family, my friends, and of course, Tom's family and friends. Being surrounded by the people we love the most is fantastic. Without your help and support, I don't think we could have got this far, and we hope you all enjoy yourselves today as much as we're going to.'

'All my friends are here tonight and I couldn't be happier to see them – although I'm not sure if they feel the same way about me, as I've been in a frenzy of pre-wedding anxiety for the last six months. Thanks girls, I really could not have done it without you. All that remains for me to say is just make sure you have a fantastic time.'

Sample speeches: Recent bereavement

'It is a great sadness that my parents cannot be here today to see Graham and me finally making it down the aisle. They both knew and loved Graham, and though neither mum nor dad ever put any pressure on us, I know it was their fondest wish that the two of us should get married in church, as we have done here today. So I'd like to dedicate this day to their memory, and to say an enormous thank you to them both for all the love and patience they showed to me and my brothers and sisters while we were growing up. And if I ever have children, and if I can do half as good a job as a parent, then I'll have done very well...'

'My mum and I were always very close, and I know that we would have spent the months leading up to this wedding busily making plans and drawing up lists and traipsing round all the dress shops comparing fabrics. So when she died last year, I thought it would be a great sadness to go through all these preparations without her. Of course, I missed her wisdom and her wit at every turn, but I had a strong sense that her presence was guiding me the whole time. So thanks for your help, mum. Anything that goes well today is down to you – I'll take credit for the mistakes!'

'At this point I'd like to take a moment to mention my best friend Katie, who cannot be here today because of a bereavement in her own family. Our thoughts are with her at this difficult time, and we send her and her family all our love and condolences.'

Toasts given by the bride

Traditionally, the bride does not make a speech, so there is no formal toast for her to make. This means she can choose to toast whomever she likes. Popular choices are her parents/groom's parents and family, her bridesmaids/helpers, absent friends, particularly if one is a parent or close relative, and/or her new husband!

Poetry in motion

'As I was searching for something to express what I want to say to Rob today, I came across a poem by another Rob, the poet Robert Browning, who wrote: "Grow old along with me! The best is yet to be." I want to thank Rob for agreeing to grow old with me and say that, after such a brilliant day, that if the best is yet to come, I can't wait! So please fill up your glasses and toast my new husband – to Robert!'

Mum's the word

'There's an old Chinese saying that to find a good wife you must look for the daughter of a great mother. After what mum and dad have organized for me today, I think we'll all agree, this is one truly great mother. And Ed and I would like to ask you to make a special toast to thank her. To mum!'

Hard labour

'Many of you might have expected my sister Claire to be my chief bridesmaid and, indeed, that was the original plan. Unfortunately she can't be here today as she's virtually in labour – now what kind of feeble excuse is that? Ladies and gentlemen, please raise your glasses to Claire, the best sister anyone could have.'

Thanks, maids

'I'd like to take this opportunity to thank my lovely bridesmaids for doing my make-up, doing my hair, arranging my bouquet, helping me with my frock and, most importantly, putting up with a complete maniac for the last six months. I promise you, I'll leave you in peace now, girls. Let's drink to them, ladies and gentlemen: The bridesmaids!'

For more sample toasts, see page 162.

The Chief Bridesmaid's Speech

Although there is a growing trend for bridesmaids to make speeches, it is neither traditional nor compulsory and will not happen at all weddings.

If the bride is making a speech, it is a nice touch for her chief bridesmaid to add a short speech to hers.

What's expected of the Chief Bridesmaid?

As chief bridesmaid or maid/matron of honour, you may wish, or be called upon, to make a speech at the reception. You have fewer compulsory elements to include, and the greater part of your speech can be about the bride, your relationship with her and her relationship with the groom. In this case it is usual for the bride to speak just before or after the groom, while the chief bridesmaid either follows or precedes the best man.

Where to start

Obviously the formality of your speech depends on the formality of the occasion, but if you are the bride's sister, or your relationship with her as a very old friend is well known, then you can get away with poking a bit more fun at her!

- Compliment the bride, and thank her for choosing you as her chief bridesmaid.
- Comment on the preparations for the wedding – this is the time you have spent together, both in the run-up to the day and in the time directly before the ceremony.
- Share a memory of the bride that highlights an amusing or endearing part of her personality.
- Compliment the ushers on behalf of the bridesmaids.
- Toast the bride and groom.

Sample speeches: Mr and Mrs

'Well, she's done it. Nicola has finally found a man who deserves her and, as one of her oldest friends, I couldn't be happier for her.

I just wanted to say a few unbiased words about what a great friend she is. No matter how far away we are physically from each other, she is always there for me and always says the right thing. I hope I can do the same for her today on her most important day. We go way back to the time when her ideal man was Action Man, all muscles and no brain. Fortunately, she's grown up since then and has chosen a man who matches her in every capacity, which is a rare thing for any couple to find.

Nicola is one of the nicest people I know, and I'm delighted to add John to my list of new friends. I hope that you'll be very happy together.

A toast – I know it's been done before, but – please raise your glasses to… the bride and groom.'

Sample speeches: She's the best

'Today I've been doing my duty as chief bridesmaid – and it's been great fun. But for years, Laura has been doing her duty as best friend. She's comforted me when I've been sobbing my eyes out over various losers, she's congratulated me when I've been promoted. We've shopped till we've dropped together, shared tonnes of chocolate and what must have been hundreds of bottles of wine. In all that time, Laura has been unfailingly kind, funny, generous and altogether one in a million. Tom, I'm sure you know it already, but let me say it again. You are a very, very lucky man.'

Sample speeches: Sister of the bride

'As Emily's younger sister, I have some advice for the groom. Peter, always treat Emily gently and with respect. Never forget to listen to her opinions and value her contribution to your marriage. Never forget that she hates milk in her coffee, that she loves roses and can't stand classical music. And above all – and I speak from bitter experience – never, ever borrow her mascara without asking.'

'I think that perhaps because I'm Emily's big sister, I sometimes worry about her. But not today. Emily has definitely found the right man in Peter and I'm happy and proud to be their chief bridesmaid.'

'Ever since she was small, my sister Emily has had a reputation for being just a teeny bit fussy about her clothes. As the chief bridesmaid who helped her get ready this morning, all I can say on the subject is that I need a drink – and I need it now!'

Sample speeches: When we were kids

'Lucy and I first met Simon at playschool. She was the only girl he'd allow in the Wendy house and he was the only boy she'd allow to play with her on the water table. It was obviously love at first sight.'

'Lucy, Simon and I all went to the same school which means I've had the dubious pleasure of seeing Simon in a cagoule. He was the sort of kid other boys looked up to. Whether it was his multi-function utility belt or his animal-print desert boots that first caught Lucy's eye, I've yet to be told.'

Sample speeches: Team spirit

'If you approach marriage with the same team spirit you've shown in all of the things we've done together, Pam, you won't go far wrong. Ever since I've known you, you've been a great team player, whether it was in the girl guides, netball or the drinking team at college. Your selflessness and determination, I'm sure, are what attracted Jonathan to you... That and the fact that you can drink most rugby players under the table...'

'I think you'll all agree that the two of them together will make an awesome team. With his drive, determination and passion for DIY, and her ability to look interested, there'll be no stopping them...'

'I look at the two of you and think to myself, what a wonderful life you have in front of you. There's no stopping you now. The only thing I would advise, Jonathan – it's an old cliché, but it's true – is never go to bed on an argument.
You never know if you're going to wake up otherwise...'

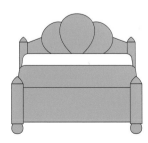

Sample speeches: Short and snappy

'Okay, John, I thought I'd make a few things clear from the start! Nicola needs to use the phone for long gossip sessions with her friends about how wonderful you are and you're expected to pick up the tab. She has the right to get annoyed when you want to watch football instead of going with her to the supermarket, where she will wander aimlessly up and down every aisle, even though you only came in for pizza to eat in front of the football. She will get grumpy once a month and you have to realize that this has nothing to do with hormones but is entirely down to you. Okay, so it isn't, but she's a woman and has the right to behave like this.

Why? Because you married her, and I'm delighted that you have. I think that the pair of you make a lovely couple and you both look stunning. It's good to see both of you make an effort for a change.

I remember the day when Nick wouldn't wear anything apart from jeans, and I have a horrible feeling that she's probably got a pair on under her dress so she can slide down the banisters later. Some things never change, even though she is a responsible bank clerk now!

So, as her best friend/sister, I'd like you to raise your glasses… to John and Nicola. May they always be as happy as they are today.'

Toasts

Raise your glass! This is your essential guide to making toasts.

No wedding would be complete without a toast to the bride and groom, accompanied by a cool sip of bubbly. Today's increasingly sophisticated wedding speeches have evolved from traditional toasts where guests drank the health of the newlyweds. And although toasts are now often only one element of a larger speech, they still have an important role to play.

What are toasts for?

Sincerity and practicality are the keys to a successful toast.
A toast that comes from the heart will only add to the
emotion of an already highly emotional day.

But toasts are of practical value, too. They can help punctuate
a day that is always hectic and complicated by alerting guests
to the end of speeches, and to the transition from one part of
the wedding day to the next.

Toasts should have a clear purpose, whether it's simply to
salute the bride and groom (usually the job of the best man)
or to honour friends and family who couldn't make it and/or
who have passed away.

Toasts can serve as a natural break in the proceedings if – as
is often the case with the best man's speech – you have gone
through a long list of thank yous or other messages. And
they're a quick and easy way to express additional thanks to
specific members of the wedding party, such as the mothers of
the bride and groom. If you are presenting gifts during a toast,
for instance to the mothers or bridesmaids, make sure you
leave time for the exchange to take place.

Dos and don'ts

Do instruct the guests as to what to do. For example:
'Please raise your glasses with me…' Give them time
to do so before you launch into the actual toast.
Do tell guests exactly what the wording of the toast is
to be, for example 'To the bride and groom' or 'The happy
couple!' etc. Clarity is the key to a good toast.
Do keep your toast focused.
Do make your toast positive or funny.
Do finish your toast with a flourish and leave them
wanting more.
Do sit when the guests sit down after the toast.

Don't rush into a toast before your guests have had time to
follow your instructions, or it will end up confused and only
half-heard.
Don't make your toast too wordy – or guests won't be able
to follow it.
Don't forget, where appropriate, to include your partner
in the toast if he/she isn't going to make a speech, for
example: 'My wife and I would like to say a special thank
you to the bridesmaids…'

Find some inspiration here with these sample toasts:

Toasts by purpose

To absent friends (from far away)

Wedding speechmakers might want to mention close relatives and good friends who can't be there on the day.

'It's wonderful to see so many of our friends and family gathered here to share Debbie and Ian's happiness. However, as you know, Shirley and Jim were sadly unable to make it over from New Zealand to be with us today. They send their very best wishes to the happy couple, and I'd like to ask you to charge your glasses and drink a toast to them, and all our other absent friends. To – absent friends!'

Absence owing to illness

'My Dad's absolutely gutted that he can't be with us today, but unfortunately he's languishing in hospital even as we speak. He keeps telling us it's his old war wound playing up, but actually that yoga class finally did for his hip. Anyway, we'll be at his bedside tomorrow with the video to cheer him up, but meanwhile let's raise our glasses to him and other absent friends.'

To absent friends (deceased)

'As you probably all know, I have the honour of speaking in place of Edward, Hayley's father, who passed away last year. All through the day, as I've looked around at everyone having such a great time, I've thought about how much Edward would have loved this wedding. Everyone who knew him will remember how much he enjoyed occasions like this – music, having fun, eating, laughing, having a drink… or two – that was the Ed we all loved. And, of course, he would have been awfully proud and awfully happy to be giving away his beloved daughter. We all miss his presence greatly, but we know that he would have wanted everyone here to have a wonderful time. That's what we intend to do, but first, let's raise our glasses and drink a toast to Edward. Ladies and gentlemen, to Edward, the father and friend we'll never forget.'

Toasts to children

The wedding is bound to be a big occasion in the lives of any children of the bride and/or groom, whether it's cementing their parents' existing relationship or marking the formation of a new family. Make the children feel part of things by offering a toast to them in your speech.

To children (of this relationship)
Lovely bridesmaid

'Of course, this is a very special day for Sam and Georgia, but it's not quite the happiest day of their lives. That day was when their lovely daughter Heather was born, and now she's taking part in her parents' big day by being their beautiful bridesmaid. Let's drink a toast to her.'

Baby boom

'Max isn't the only man in Laura's life. There's also their baby son Louis, for whom they're not just the bride and groom, they're the best mum and dad in the world. Will you all join me in raising your glasses to Louis, and may the whole family have many happy days ahead. To Louis and all the family!'

To children (of a previous relationship)
Father figure
'Sarah hasn't just gained a husband in Tom, Leo has also gained a stepdad. Luckily for both of them, Tom shares Leo's love of Curly-Wurlys and computer games, as well as his interest in cars, Star Wars films and, more puzzlingly, the fortunes of Manchester City. Here's to many hours of shivering in the stands together – Tom and Leo.'

Mothering matters
'Harry didn't only fall in love with Helen because she's such good fun. He could also see what a great mum she is by the way she has brought up her daughter Alice and son Joe. They are fantastic kids and a real credit to her, so it's not surprising that Harry couldn't stop himself from falling in love with them, too. Now they're all together as one family, and we wish them lots of love- and laugh-filled days to come. So please raise your glasses and drink a toast to Helen and Harry – and Alice and Joe.'

For second marriages

Second marriage speeches can be tricky, so be tactful when you make your toast. Always check your words out with a close family member first.

Voice of experience

'There was once a very famous and successful Avis car rental advertising campaign that simply said: "We're number two. We try harder." Well, this may be marriage number two for this happy couple but, like Avis, they're sure to turn their experience to their advantage. So please raise your glasses to the bride and groom!'

Second chance of happiness

'Sue and Colin are so good together that it's hardly surprising that they've decided to give marriage another try. All weddings are special occasions, but perhaps this one is even more so, because it represents a second chance of happiness for both of them – and they've decided to grab it with both hands. Good luck to them! Please raise your glasses to the happy couple and wish them all the very best for the future. To the happy couple!'

To the happy couple

These examples may help if you're asked to speak at
a wedding where there are no formal speeches, or at a
rehearsal dinner.

'Let's hope that the two of you live as long as you like.
And let's hope you have all you like for as long as you live...'

'I'm a person who likes to use simple words to say simple
things. But before I ask these fine people to raise their glasses
to the happy couple, I'd just like to say: congratulations on the
termination of your isolation. May I express an appreciation of
your determination to end the desperation and frustration
that has caused you so much consternation. It's such good
news that you've been given inspiration to make a
combination to bring an accumulation to the population.
Cheers to the happy couple!'

'I know that, from this day forward, the best days of your past
will be the worst days of your future. Together, you're going to
have the happiest life imaginable. To the bride and groom!'

'Being a person of very few words, I give you the bride
and groom.'

'Here's to the happy couple. Remember, you two, that you should always view your marriage as if it were a pair of scissors. What I mean by that is that you cannot be separated, even though you're often moving in opposite directions. To the happy couple!'

'My advice to the happy couple is to live life as if today is your last day on earth together, and that when tomorrow comes it's simply an added bonus. Here's to today and plenty more bonuses to come – the bride and groom!'

'Just a quick word from me to the bride and groom. Here's to the bride and here's to the groom, all newly wed. May all their troubles be light as bubbles or as feathers that make up their bed!'

'Here's to the newlyweds. Let's just hope that, when push comes to shove, your "for better or for worse" turns out to be far better than worse.'

'Here's to love, laughter and happy ever after. As Rob and Julie start their wedded life, here's to the fabulous new husband and wife.'

'Here's to the health of the bride.
Here's to the health of the groom.
Here's to the ones who tied the knot.
And to the rest of you here, whom I haven't forgot!'

To the parents/grandparents
'Here's to the few who made this crew. To the grandparents!'

'To the greatest grandparents. I've got a feeling that you might be great-grandparents very soon!'

To the bride from the groom
'I'd like you all to fill your glasses and toast Mary, my bride and joy!'

'With every passing day that I've known you, you've got more and more beautiful. But looking at you today, my darling, you already look like tomorrow.'

'Here's to you and here's to me. Let's hope we never disagree. Here's to our families and our honoured guests. And here's to you never wearing those horrid string vests.

Confetti.co.uk is the UK's leading wedding and special occasion website, helping more than 400,000 brides, grooms and guests every month.

Confetti.co.uk is packed full of ideas and advice to help organize every stage of your wedding. At Confetti, you can choose from hundreds of beautiful wedding dresses; investigate our list of more than 3,000 wedding and reception venues; plan your wedding; chat to other brides about their experiences and ask for advice from Aunt Betti our agony aunt. If your guests are online, too, we will even help you set up a wedding website to share details and photos with your family and friends.

Our extensive online content on every aspect of weddings and special occasions is now complemented by our range of books covering every aspect of planning a wedding, for everyone involved. Titles include *Wedding Planner; How to Write a Wedding Speech; The Best Man's Speech; The Best Man's Wedding; The Groom's Wedding; The Bride's Wedding; The Father of the Bride's Wedding; Your Daughter's Wedding; The Bridesmaid's Wedding; Getting Married Abroad; The Wedding Book of Calm; Wedding Readings & Vows* and *Wedding Readings.*

Confetti also offer:
Wedding and special occasion stationery – our stunning ranges include all the pieces you will need for all occasions, including christenings, namings, anniversaries and birthday parties.
Wedding and party products – stocking everything you need from streamers to candles to cameras to cards to flowers to fireworks and, of course, confetti!

To find out more or to order your Confetti gift book, party brochure or wedding stationery brochure visit: www.confetti.co.uk
call: 0870 840 6060; email: info@confetti.co.uk
visit: Confetti, 80 Tottenham Court Road, London W1T 4TE
or Confetti, The Light, The Headrow, Leeds LS1 8TL